A PRISTINE SUICIDE

By Bart J. Allen

From the Publisher:
This book was published in the hopes of finding the truth about the death of Destry Allen. All claims and/or opinions contained in the book are those of the author and do not necessarily reflect those of the publisher and staff.

"A Pristine Suicide," by Bart J. Allen. ISBN 978-1-60264-162-4 (softcover); 978-1-60264-163-1 (hardcover); 978-1-60264-165-5 (electronic).

Library of Congress Control Number: 2011912418.

Published 2011 by Virtualbookworm.com Publishing Inc., P.O. Box 9949, College Station, TX 77842, US. ©2011, Bart J. Allen. All rights reserved. No part of this publication may be reproduced, stored in a retrieval system, or transmitted in any form or by any means, electronic, mechanical, recording or otherwise, without the prior written permission of Bart J. Allen.

Manufactured in the United States of America.

Dedicated to those that knew and loved
Destry Greer Allen,
and the truth.

September 17, 1986 – June 10, 2004

Pristine: pris tine   [pris-teen, pri-steen] –adjective

1. having its original purity; uncorrupted or unsullied.
2. of or pertaining to the earliest period or state; primitive.

Chapter 1

The beginning of summer is always a highly anticipated time, but the fact of the matter was June was a dreaded month around the Allen house. Kids are giddy to be out of school with a whole summer ahead. Summer jobs, socializing, doing anything but going to school. Parents are busy planning, trying to come up with activities to keep the kids busy, out of trouble and out of their hair. In Salina, Kansas, the longest days of the year are getting sticky hot.

Unfortunately, June had historically brought some type of medical emergency to our house. My wife, Theresa, had four separate surgeries – an emergency appendectomy, a ruptured ovarian cyst with accompanying artery, and two cervical spine surgeries – in three different years. My mother had also died in June after a mercifully brief battle with cancer. Though nobody in the household really believed a month could influence such random events, as the month rolled around each year, it didn't keep us from joking about whether we would survive another June.

The morning of Thursday, June 10, 2004 didn't seem different. I was up and getting myself and the house ready for the day. As eight o'clock neared, I went to check on Destry, our oldest son, to make sure he was getting ready for work. He had a summer job pulling weeds, painting and other such odd jobs at the company I worked for. Destry was excited about the anticipated cash flow the next couple of months would bring and though he was generally very good about getting up on his own, every now and then a secondary alarm system, me or his mother, was needed.

Upon entering his room, it was immediately apparent he wasn't there, though both the bedroom and bathroom lights were on. On occasion, Destry would get up early and visit his girlfriend, Nichole, before other planned activities, such as work. They were very close to one another and though his mother and I were unsure quite what to make of the relationship itself, it impressed us that anything could get a seventeen-year-old boy up at dawn on his own accord. In fact, the term close doesn't really do justice to their relationship, at least from Destry's perspective. Nichole was everything. Finding him gone first thing in the morning was a little troublesome, but certainly not unexplainable.

I expected that I would find him at work when I got there so I didn't mention his absence to his mother. I didn't think it was a big deal. Destry was a big boy, soon to be a senior in high school, so if he wanted to get up early and see his girlfriend before work, it was really his business, though he was certainly expected to tell us first and up until now, always did.

The absence of Destry's car was immediately obvious as I arrived at work. I was mildly miffed and surprised that he wasn't honoring his commitment but not overly concerned. I say surprised because if nothing else, and unlike many young men his age, Destry was very reliable and dependable. However, I was also aware that young love can often throw a wrench into the most carefully laid plans.

I immediately called Destry's cell phone but it went unanswered. Though I would have preferred he answer the call, I was also aware that upon seeing I was calling, he would more than likely remember the time and where he was supposed to be. Why answer the phone to get your butt chewed? Just get to where you are supposed to be, work up a good excuse and take the butt chewing later. I certainly understood the logic. I checked with those at work that would know whether he had been there and left but nobody had seen him. I left word that I was going to go look for him and would return shortly.

I returned home, entertaining the possibility that time got away from him and, for whatever reason, he needed to return home to prepare for work and would arrive late. He wasn't there, so I turned around and drove back to work, thinking he had possibly gone straight to work after my reminder call. Though this sounds cumbersome, the company I worked for was only about five minutes away from where we lived. Again, his car wasn't there. I called him again and again, no answer. I returned home hoping I had just missed him in all of the commuting. Again, Destry wasn't there.

Salina puts on an event known as The Smoky Hill River Festival every year at centrally located Oakdale Park. Volunteers are always welcomed and Destry had spent the previous afternoon working with others to set up the festival for the coming weekend. The festival is a much anticipated event and many help year after year. Like the other workers, Destry enjoyed the tradition and becoming a part of it.

It occurred to me that possibly I had misunderstood his work schedule at the festival. Maybe he was to work there in the morning hours. As I sat in my car, I called the two people that Destry had worked for the day before, but neither had seen him. The park is a pretty big place, but both of the individuals had known Destry since he was a boy and would certainly recognize him if they saw him. There weren't that many volunteers that early in the morning and, at nearly six foot five inches with red hair, he would be hard to miss, even from a distance.

I racked my brain for other possibilities. One time, Destry had spent the night at a friend's house. He didn't ever do that sort of thing and it was suspicious. We allowed it but believed it was really some sort of ruse to spend the night with Nichole. I drove by the place, but his car wasn't there.

At this point, I began to get worried. I again tried to call him to no avail. I remember sitting at a traffic signal entertaining very disturbing scenarios, trying to tell myself not to let my imagination get away from me. He couldn't be found, he wouldn't answer his phone and I was running out of places to look.

In the not too distant past, a young man in Salina had his truck carjacked, with him as a passenger. The scumbags took him to a nearby reservoir, tried to hack him to death with a machete, then ran over him with his own truck for good measure. After all that work, they then set the vehicle afire. Incredibly, the guy lived and the bad guys were caught.

The mind is a disturbingly active place at times. Destry had just gotten a "new" used car, a 2000 230 C class Mercedes, and it was this vehicle that he was missing in. Though a relatively inexpensive car, especially used, many of the class sensitive believe all Mercedes are expensive and an indicator of wealth. Could someone have carjacked Destry last night? I sat there telling myself that things like that just don't happen, especially twice. That stuff happens to other people, everyone knows that. I decided to drive back to work to check again. Still, no Destry. Again, I drove home, with the same results.

I started trying to think a little more creatively. Not just where could he be at this time of day, but where could he be at anytime. Nichole worked at a local lumber yard and sometimes had to be at work at 8 a.m. Perhaps he was out there, his phone was dead and he was unaware of the time. It was worth checking out since driving back and forth to work seemed pointless and I had to do something. This was all so totally uncharacteristic of Destry.

As I left the house towards the lumber yard, my mind was still churning. Though it was certainly a possibility that Destry was there, I didn't really believe it. As I got to the intersection to turn towards the lumber yard, it suddenly occurred to me that possibly Destry had gone out to a place we have just outside of town, known as the Depot. I could think of absolutely no reason why on earth he would be out there, but it was as likely, or unlikely, as the lumber yard and closer. In fact, from the intersection I was sitting at, it was only two miles down the very street I was facing. Rather than turn right, I headed left towards the Depot.

From a distance, I could see the chain that was normally locked across the driveway was down. It seemed the riddle was solved. I was relieved to know where he was, but why was he here? I turned into the long drive and as the Depot came into sight, I spotted his car, confirming that he was indeed the visitor to the property. My first thought was that he and Nichole had come out late at night, fallen asleep and failed to wake up. The Depot is buried deep in the woods and perpetually in the shadows, but I found it hard to believe they could sleep in three hours past dawn, especially knowing they were expected to be elsewhere.

I was a little irritated at the situation, mostly because it was so terribly inconsistent with Destry's normal behavior. It would be hard to explain getting caught in bed with his girlfriend and blowing off his obligations to work. I approached the front door and found the screen door nearly torn off its hinges, a detail I unfortunately wouldn't remember for some time afterward.

I was getting more than a little irritated now. Not only were they blowing off work and sleeping in, for some reason they broke the screen door. The main door was closed, with Destry's keys hanging in the lock, though it wasn't locked. As I opened the door, I immediately looked to my left and up toward the end of the building where there was an open loft with an inflatable bed. I didn't get a chance to see if they were up there. My eyes immediately fell upon the table surrounded by folding chairs that was between me and the loft. I always remember what I thought next as a 1-2-3-snap.

One: The first footstep. I didn't leave the gun lying on the table. I kept a .22 caliber revolver hidden on top of the kitchen cabinet in the Depot, not in the middle of a table.

Two: The second footstep. The revolver was laying near a small pool of blood on the tabletop. Well, maybe it's not too bad, but then I glimpse feet protruding out the side of the table I'm standing by.

Three: The third footstep. I see Destry laying face down in a large pool of blood and body fluids. He's discolored, his nose and mouth covered in pulmonary edema foam, lack of respiration obvious. He's dead. Destry had left in the middle of the night and we didn't get to say goodbye.

SNAP. I heard it as clearly as a branch breaking. I don't know what it meant and don't expect I probably ever will. I immediately began muttering "Oh God" over and over and over in one long sentence, who knows how many times.

My first thought was that maybe it was a murder-suicide, or a suicide-suicide, and I immediately stepped over the mess to go up into the loft. This act alone is a clear indication that I was assuming that Destry and Nichole were together the night before and that something had gone terribly, terribly wrong. It disturbs me to this day that my first response was to check to see if my son had murdered someone else before murdering himself. Such is the power of overwhelming, debilitating shock.

Upon finding the loft empty, I descended and approached the table. The gun was laid upon the picture, which was itself partially covering a trail of blood droplets that went to the edge of the table. The scene immediately caused my mind to come to a startling and singular conclusion. I was shocked to discover a person could shoot themselves in the head and then still have the wherewithal to set the gun down in a purposeful manner. This was inconceivable to me. I reached for the pistol to see if it had been shot more than once. I have no idea why this mattered. As I put my hand forward, a voice in my head, as clear as if someone had screamed it into my ear, demanded "Don't touch the gun! It's a crime scene!" I pulled my hand back immediately.

While my having knowledge of the effects of such wounds may sound strange to the casual observer, it's instructive to know that I've hunted all of my life and, as such, have observed many animals dying from head wounds. Additionally, I've seen pigs, cows, and horses shot between the eyes and the result is quite predictable. They don't look for a place to fall or go carefully to their knees. They instantaneously drop to the ground. All the video images I've digested of people being executed by various nauseating regimes of the twentieth century show the same thing.

The point is that if Destry could set the gun down in a way that he wanted it to be found after having shot himself in the head, he would have had time to suffer. That bothered me a lot.

The whole situation is instructive as to the state of shock, bewilderment, and gullibility I was experiencing overall. Suffice at this point to say, part of the conclusion I came to was correct. The scene on the table was specifically set up and a person that has been shot nearly between the eyes, as an examination by law enforcement would later reveal, can't formulate a thought or action. They're instantly unconscious. That then leaves the question of how the scene got that way if it simply wasn't possible for the shooting victim to do it. Unfortunately, in my fragile state of mind, that didn't occur to me. I simply doubted myself, years of firsthand knowledge, and, worse yet, my son, who had always been consistently critical of suicide as a solution to life's problems.

My thoughts returned to finding Nichole, for some reason convinced that she was with him, even though I knew somewhere in my mind she drove home in her own car from our house. I walked outside to confront seemingly endless woods. If she was out there, I wouldn't be able to find her. All of a sudden it occurred to me to call her. Maybe she hadn't been with him after all. Though I didn't have her phone number, I did have her mom's.

It took more time than usual to call her mom since I suddenly found I was unable to use my phone. Though it seemed to me I was thinking and acting pretty clearly, in truth, my mind was failing to function correctly. Standing there staring at my phone, I was literally unable to remember how to work the damn thing. To say it was a frustrating moment would be a gross understatement. Finally, I got my mind to focus. I called, spoke with her mom and asked her to have Nichole call me, which she did right away. Having confirmed she was alright, she inquired why I was looking for her. I replied I couldn't find Destry and was at least trying to find her. She knew nothing and I told her I would call her later.

I hung up, believing in my shell shocked mind that she had done something terrible and Destry came to the woods to kill himself, alone. It's strange what the mind comes up with in times of extreme stress. For instance, I don't remember making any sort of decision to begin screaming at the top of my lungs until I couldn't breathe anymore. It just happened. Oddly though, I do remember thinking that the workers at the grain elevator a half mile away could probably hear me.

Chapter 2

The next few days were, as one would expect, a nightmare. The Saline County Sheriff's Office (SO) declared they were confident it was a suicide, so much so that they weren't even going order the autopsy that is required by law on any minor that dies, especially in a suspicious manner and unattended. They informed us that we were certainly welcome to have one done ourselves at our own expense. This all simply reinforced the belief that Destry had killed himself. Hell, the authorities were so certain they were willing to break the law and even told us they were going to do it.

My concern at the time was primarily getting my son's body back for his mother and getting on as quickly as possible with the horrendous business. I am the first to admit that I may not have made wise decisions at the time and placed my trust in law enforcement. That won't happen again. We didn't have an autopsy done, had the body cremated and prepared for the memorial service.

Even though we tried to accept what we were told, a couple of things didn't make sense and by the time the memorial service was conducted four days later, we had some doubts about the official story. These doubts were enough that we discouraged the pastor from working the suicide angle too much at the memorial service.

Out of instinct I guess, I called my dad the day I found Destry and had him come out to the Depot where I broke the news to him. I asked him to stay while I went into town to inform Theresa, Destry's mother, and then called law enforcement. He was on the scene when authorities got there up until they left. As it happened, he was given some information about the scene that would eventually be very significant.

Dr. Allred, the Saline County Coroner, had announced to my dad at the scene that it was a "pristine suicide". A suicide in its uncorrupted, native state? He also began to talk about the disposition of the body, at which point my dad abruptly stopped him, stating that Dr. Allred was talking to the wrong person. He needed to talk to the parents. Dr. Allred replied there was nothing to talk about. The body would have an autopsy because it was state law. End of discussion.

Several things were puzzling about the scene. For one thing, as mentioned Destry was laying face down on the floor. When his body was rolled over, his class ring was found on the floor in close proximity to his left hand, which was under his body. What was of interest was that the ring normally was found on the ring finger of Destry's right hand. How did it get off his finger on the floor under his body, near his left hand? Destry had a habit of playing with his ring, continually pulling it off and on his finger with his left hand when he was sitting around. Was he playing with his ring when whatever it was happened?

Another point related to us by my dad upon leaving the scene and returning to the house was that, as reported to him by the SO, Destry was shot nearly between the eyes. I found what he was saying surprising. I had assumed when I was at the scene the he had been shot in the temple. At one point, I actually looked into Destry's face from less than two feet away and saw no wound, though admittedly the blood and fluids obscured much of his face, as well as the scene in general. Presumably, Destry shot himself point blank. Such a wound would leave a powder burn on the skin and I hadn't seen any such indication when I looked into his face.

I'm sure most would wonder why in the world I would believe I was even vaguely qualified to classify gunshot as point-blank wounds or not. Strangely enough, several years before Destry's death, one of the guys at work committed suicide by shooting himself between the eyes in anticipation of being sent to jail. I went to visit the poor guy at the funeral home and was quite flabbergasted to find that an eight point stellar tattoo was quite clearly visibly seared into the skin. Even though the body had been cleaned and make up had been applied liberally, they were unable to remove it or completely obscure it. It was a memorable learning moment for me.

Between the class ring and what I remembered as a lack of powder searing of the skin, we came to the initial conclusion that he may have accidentally shot himself while taking the ring off. It seemed unlikely that anyone would try to shoot themselves between the eyes by holding the gun a distance from their head, while at the same time hold onto a ring. Why wouldn't they just put the gun to their head and eliminate the possibility of only wounding themselves by holding the gun out and away?

Of course, there was no way to know this for sure. Ultimately, in situations such as ours, the question quickly comes down to this one point. The fact of the matter is that when a person is alone and dies from a gunshot, nobody can say for absolute certainty what really happened. Many times it may seem obvious, but those last few moments can never truly be known. That is also why law enforcement always assumes the death to be a homicide, unless proven otherwise. At least that's how it happens in places other than Salina.

Suicide or accidental self-inflicted death? That seemed to be the question in our case. Of course, there was one other possibility – homicide. But since the SO said in no uncertain terms it was a suicide, we literally didn't even discuss it. Unfortunately, the question of suicide versus accident is ultimately six of one and a half dozen of the other. Since there are no witnesses in the final moments, it's a question that can often not be answered to the satisfaction of all parties. As such, we continued on with the memorial service but felt we needed to downplay the suicide angle. To many, I'm sure this sounds like denial of reality and I would be the first to admit it as a possibility except for one thing.

As mentioned previously, I've hunted all of my life. One thing I've found out over the years is that if a person is around firearms enough, eventually they will almost get shot or will almost shoot themselves or someone else. Ask any hunter and they will relate a story of near death at the hands of themselves or a dear friend because of an errant shot or because they forgot to unload the gun when they put it in the car. Just ask Dick Cheney.

Destry accidentally shooting himself made at least as much sense as what we were being told. Destry thought suicide was a way out of life intended to hurt those left standing. He had no suicidal ideations and didn't suffer from any overwhelming depression. In fact, if anything he was really excited about life and at the top of his young game. He and Nichole had a meaningful talk that night and he couldn't wait to get back to the festival the next day. Plus, it was the hallowed last summer, that time between junior and senior year in high school when it occurs to students that the end is finally near. As of the last day of school all juniors are automatically elevated to senior status, regardless of the fact school isn't in session. Finally, the top of the heap.

There were other things that seemed contrary to the suicidal mindset. The way his room was left seemed to indicate he intended on returning. Not only were all the lights on, acne medication was laid out in preparation to take first thing in the morning. His car was backed in to the parking space when he parked at the depot and the keys left in the ignition, just as it always was.

The picture that was left on the table turned out to be relatively insignificant according to Nichole. Destry only had it because Nichole had brought it over to him that night. It wasn't even a picture he liked in particular. Nichole also mentioned that Destry knew of the gun and was curious about it since she didn't think he had ever actually shot it.

A lot of questions that had no answers it seemed and at the end of the day we were left with only one inescapable fact. Our son was dead, no matter how it happened and our lives were not going to be the same. We limped through the rest of the summer attempting to carry on, but we were determined to answer whatever questions could be.

The first thing seemed to be getting a copy of the report from the SO. Far from being helpful to the grieving family, they did everything they could to stand in our way. They actually forced us to get a court order in order to see the report they generated about our son's death. Initially, we believed they were just acting in the typically arrogant manner of Salina cops, legendary in central Kansas. Why would our son's death be any of our business?

Nonetheless, nearly two months after Destry's death, we obtained the reports, gruesome photos and all. I had been at the scene and knew what to expect, but the details I had forgotten astounded me. For myself, I felt it necessary that if I was going to be forced to remember a scene such as that for the rest of my life, I wanted to remember it accurately.

Not really eager to be seen as a crazy parent by anyone, including our attorney, I felt it was necessary that I study the photos and reports for clues and inconsistencies and come up with a legitimate list before asking others to get involved. Hysterically implying our son couldn't have possibly done something like this certainly wasn't going to be productive.

As we started digging through all of the reports and photos, several disturbing details became immediately crystal clear. Literally, no investigation was ever conducted by the SO, information was withheld from us and worst of all, they lied. They never asked anyone about why the screen door was nearly ripped from its hinges. I had been at the Depot the day before Destry died and the door was fine. Due to shock, presumably, until the photos jogged my memory, I had forgotten that the screen door was completely broken and the screen fabric torn when I arrived at the scene.

To put this in perspective, imagine you arrive home to find your spouse shot dead and the front door has been violently broken since you were last at home yesterday. I think most would find it hard to believe that the only logical conclusion would be that the victim killed themselves.

The door was just the beginning. Analysis of the table top where the suicide supposedly took place created more questions than answers. The more I studied the photos, the more I realized that what I was looking at was basically a macabre Norman Rockwell painting. Those that are familiar with Rockwell's work will know what I'm talking about.

Rockwell paintings, at the risk of oversimplifying, embody the old adage that a picture is worth ten thousand words. Rockwell specialized in depicting Americana at its most endearing. His most popular works were almost always scenes of common familiarity with intricate detail that told a warm, common story. At the same time, most admirers of his work realize the scenes he illustrates are typically quite idealistic and seldom encountered in the all too real world.

The table top was graphic. It was also too perfectly set up to be true, much like a Rockwell painting. It appeared as a person might believe it should look, not as it would look in the real world. There's a huge difference. As I mentioned before, even before I reviewed photos, I remembered that one of my first impressions was I was astounded that someone shot in the head could then consciously set the gun down the way they wanted it found. Now that my brain was intact again, I realized they couldn't.

There were other observable problems. How did blood get on the gun? The gun had blood on both sides of the barrel, even though the portion of the barrel with the blood wasn't in the path of the blood trail, and there were no droplets underneath. The blood trail indicated the direction Destry fell away from the table after bleeding enough to cause a pool about four inches in diameter. It also indicated he didn't fall over from his seated position in the slumped position, but rather was moving straight backward when falling. So he shot himself slumped forward, bled and then attempted to sit upright while simultaneously falling sideways?

There was more. The picture was facing the wrong direction, under the gun but on top of the trail of blood droplets. The gun was laid down in such a way that Destry would have had to pull his hand from under the gun as he fell out of the chair and at the same time drag the photo across the blood trail, but not smear the blood with his arm which was presumably dragging the photo, all as he fell to the floor. A crucial point to remember is that the blood trail had to be there first before anything could be laid over it or dragged through it. His body was also nearly perpendicular to and completely under the table even though the blood trail on the table indicated he was falling sideways as he cleared the table.

As far as I was concerned, nothing on the table could be explained. One of the main reasons we wanted to see the photos and reports was due to my memory, or more accurately my lack of memory, of the appearance of the wound in Destry's forehead. A contact wound should have left what is commonly referred to as a powder burn. In overly simple terms, when a gun is discharged against an object, such as skin, the super-heated gases created by the burning gunpowder leave the barrel and sear whatever they touch. These gases actually exit the barrel ahead of the bullet, as well as behind it as they propel the bullet forward. The burns created by these searing gases can't be removed by washing.

My memory was confirmed. There didn't appear to be any tattooing around Destry's head wound. However, what I did observe and conclude about the wound left me feeling instantly nauseous. Upon close analysis, a faint gray ring could be made out encircling the bullet hole. I recognized this immediately. It was made by the soot residue on the end of the gun barrel. When a gun is shot repeatedly, soot created by the burning gunpowder exiting the gun collects on the end of the barrel. Anyone that has used and been around guns is aware that if the end of the gun barrel in put up against an object and rotated, it will leave a perfect circle of soot. Unlike searing caused by burning gunpowder, soot is easily removed by washing or wiping.

Indeed, the pictures showed that the soot ring was gone after the body was washed at the morgue. What disturbed me was this.

There was no tattoo indicating the gun was fired in contact with the skin, yet there was a soot ring indicating the barrel had indeed been in contact with the skin at some point.

One possible explanation would be that Destry put the gun to his head, causing the soot ring, but the gun was away from his head when the actual shot was fired. Since the soot ring was perfectly centered around the wound, that would mean Destry fired the shot away from his head but managed to perfectly center the bullet in the soot ring. Not only is it impossible, why go to all that trouble when you could just shoot yourself and be done with it? Despondent people are seldom interested in such intricacies.

The only other explanation was much more ominous but much more likely. If the soot ring didn't get on his forehead before the shot, it was put there after the shot. Obviously, Destry couldn't have done that. The only explanation was that someone else put it to his head after he was shot, in an attempt to make it appear as though the gun was at his head when discharged.

My conclusion was singular and unmistakable. The whole case suddenly made chilling sense. Destry was murdered. Realizing that no one listens to the parents of suicide victims, we instructed our attorney in K.C., Tom, that we wanted to have the photos analyzed by a professional forensic pathologist of his choosing and that we would leave it all to him so we couldn't be accused of a biased investigation and conclusion.

The written reports created by the investigators from the SO detailed an even more disturbing revelation. Contrary to what the SO had told me and my father, the last person Destry spoke with was not his girlfriend. It was his cousin, Ray Jones. Not only that, Ray was never even questioned. He had never mentioned this phone call to anyone, even though he had been at the house nearly daily since the death. In the initial days after Destry was found, Ray was quick to chime in with what he knew about the night. He just forgot to mention that particular detail.

Had the omission been by anyone else in the family but Ray, we would have initially given them the benefit of the doubt. Unfortunately, Ray had used up whatever benefits he had accrued many years before. Ray was, in his own words, the black sheep of the family.

Chapter 3

The Allen family consisted of my father and mother, Jim and Janice Allen, myself, and two sisters, Brenda and Jennifer. Theresa Miller and I married and had three sons: Destry, Ransom, and Lucas. Brenda married Kim Jones and gave birth to Raymond Wesley Jones in 1985, about a year and a half before Destry and, as cousins in the same town, became buddies. All of the holidays were family affairs and Ray was seldom absent. After his parents got divorced during his early childhood, however, things began going downhill for Ray.

Though both Brenda and Kim both lived in Salina after the divorce, Brenda's long standing but as of yet undiagnosed mental instability began to wreak havoc, most dramatically on Ray's life. At first, Kim tried to put in some effort, until the whole situation seemed to just wear him down. Suffice to say, Ray graduated into his teen years without the prerequisites necessary to lead a successful life. He was unaccountable and completely untrustworthy. Simply put, he was a prolific liar, thief and cheat.

A typical experience was as follows. On one occasion, several silver dollars were missing from the table after Ray visits, as well as a crisp, unfolded two dollar bill from a drawer. When confronted with incontrovertible evidence he was to blame, his explanation was that he just found the silver dollars laying there and simply didn't realize they belonged to anyone. After all, they didn't have a sign on them. As for the two dollar bill, he was adamant he didn't know how it got in his pocket and he found it as confusing as everyone else.

Why only accept partial responsibility? Because explaining how you just found the money in the drawer you were going through was even too much of a stretch for Ray to believe he could sell as an innocent mistake. A two-tiered lie by a twelve year old. It was an ominous signal of things to come.

Once I informed my sister, Brenda, what was going on, she convinced him to come clean and the next day they came over and Ray apologized. His lips said yes, but his eyes said no. If he was sorry for anything, it was that he got caught and called out on a lie.

Most disturbing about this very typical example was that Ray actually expected people to believe him. He was utterly unable to accept responsibility for the fact he stole money or lied constantly. When I was trying to extract a confession from him, he actually shushed me while he was pantomiming suddenly having discovered the mystical, unfolded two dollar bill in his pocket. He repeated the motions over and over. He just couldn't figure it out.

On another occasion, when riding somewhere with his father, he happened to spy a guitar amplifier under a bush near their house. They stopped and picked it up. I suggested to Kim that Ray should take it to the police department since someone was obviously missing the amp when he asked me what they should do with it. Besides, persons turning in wayward property get to keep it after a certain amount of time if nobody comes forward to claim it.

I showed up to take Ray and the amp to the police station, but he refused to answer the door. He later told me he was a heavy sleeper. The whole thing hadn't worked out quite the way

Ray had envisioned. You see his plan was that he was supposed to innocently notice the amp and get to keep it. Ray knew just showing up to the house with the amp would only raise questions, but if he just happened to find it with a witness, the result would be the same with less hassle – a free amp.

The fact was that he was most likely the one who stole it and put it under the bush in the first place to be mysteriously found at a later date. Taking it to the cops with his name attached could quite possibly have negative consequences.

That was always the case in mysteries involving Ray. It was always simply poor communications, misunderstandings, incorrect interpretations, failed memories, etc. Like all the bad things that would eventually happen involving Ray Jones, the money incident and the amp were just honest mistakes, errors, and subject to interpretation.

During Ray's teenage years, we seldom saw him other than at the occasional holiday or family get together. Quite frankly, his demeanor was so creepy and his level of trustworthiness so low that we dreaded seeing him. A visit by Ray to our house meant we needed to make sure anything of value was hidden and he couldn't be left alone, no matter what.

Even when playing with the boys, he had to be watched. Kids had a bad habit of getting hurt around Ray and, additionally, ideas to do stupid things suddenly became abundant when he came to the house. On at least four occasions, he "accidentally" broke keepsakes of Destry's obtained on family travels, travels that didn't include Ray.

At school, Ray would identify Destry's friends, then leverage his relationship as Destry's cousin to take advantage of them. This obviously didn't reflect well on Destry. He got sick and tired of it and began to limit contact with Ray. It seemed people only existed to be taken advantage of, family included.

One thing had become increasingly obvious. Ray also suffered from some sort of an apparent mental instability. He was a pathological liar. He even lied when he didn't have to lie. He lacked any semblance of a conscience. He obsessed over certain girls to the point they considered him a stalker and feared for their safety. He constantly spoke of going to medical school when, in reality, he was in danger of flunking out or being expelled. I used to openly joke with our sons that one of them should go into psychiatry and use Ray for their post-graduate work.

Nonetheless, at the time I felt bad for Ray and would pointedly try to give him some direction, though he certainly didn't ask. I only offered because it was so patently obvious he either was completely incapable of using his head or nobody had ever suggested he should, maybe both. At the time, I wasn't sure which. As far as he was concerned, everything was going great. It seemed the horizon was filled as far as the eye could see with gullible dupes.

In the early summer of 2000, one event dramatically worsened his situation. My mother, Janice Allen, was diagnosed with cancer and died, literally, within a matter of weeks after diagnosis. As Ray's grandmother, my mom was his most consistent supporter and spent a significant amount of her time and money trying to make up for what his parents wouldn't or couldn't afford. She was one of the only people consistently in his life that had expectations of at least a degree of accountability in return for her guidance and love.

However, even my mom had finally gotten worn out. In a brutally honest moment of clarity, such as one usually only experiences by the specter of death on the doorstep, in one of her last instructions to Brenda she explicitly instructed her not to waste any more of her limited resources on Ray. As far as my mom was concerned, Ray was a lost cause. It may sound harsh, but she spoke the truth. Mom didn't have any time left for mincing words. Brenda agreed wholeheartedly and vowed that she was done with him. For his part, Ray saw the family's focus on mom's rapidly approaching death as an opportunity to take advantage while everyone's guard was down.

Ray's behavior eventually became so erratic that working with him in hopes of creating a decent person was past frustrating and seemed hopeless. We saw him even less after mom died since the unity of family gatherings suffered after her death. As in many families, she was the glue. In addition, Ray didn't particularly like being around me because I required at least a modicum of truth and accountability, something he was completely unable to deliver on. For our part, we didn't want him around at all. He was a terrible influence. His victims seldom even realized what part they played in his various schemes until after the fact. Ray was bad news all the way around. One event in the spring of his junior year really cemented our fears.

Theresa received a call one evening from the mother of a girl, a senior, asking very pointedly that we keep Ray away from her daughter. This mother stated that Ray was pressuring her daughter to stop playing her violin and quit participating in school activities so she could spend her time with him. More disturbing was the fact he would just appear behind her daughter in parking lots and other places having seemingly appeared from nowhere.

Theresa was confused. We hadn't even seen Ray in several months and we certainly had no ability, legally or otherwise, to control his actions. The woman seemed in shock. Ray had apparently represented our family as his own, to the point that this woman had come to the conclusion that he actually lived with us. He spoke of no other relations.

This event was the first of several that made us aware that Ray was actively using the Allen family reputation to gain access to households he never would otherwise. The girl involved in the foregoing incident was gorgeous, smart, involved in school activities and financially well off, everything that Ray wasn't. In fact, he was the opposite. He lacked any degree of respectability or class, lied, cheated, and preyed on the trusting. However, the Allen family was known as decent, hardworking, and trustworthy and simply mentioning that he was related to us deferred some degree of credibility on him. We avoided him even more.

Ray seemed to have no redeeming virtue. To his classmates he had become a joke. He was known as a wannabe that constantly lied, cheated, stole, and was openly laughed at. Several disturbing events made it clear that the previous troubling incident with the senior girl wasn't an isolated instance. In fact, while researching this book, I was informed that one girl's parents actually filed stalking charges against him. Whether it actually happened, I don't know, but it wouldn't have been a surprise. During the spring of his junior year in high school, I earnestly suggested to his parents that what money was put away for Ray's college education would be put to better use by sending him to a military school.

I even spent time researching which schools best fit the bill for what Ray needed. My basic belief was that many of Ray's problems were due in great part to a lack of accountability for his actions. Without doubt, Ray was a slippery kid under the arrangement in place. A military school would, hopefully, change that. Interestingly, it was reported to me that Ray thought it was a great idea and actually was looking forward to the experiencet. He had also told me when we met he thought it was a great idea, but I was at the point I never knew when to believe him.

Neither of his parents had any interest in my proposal. They were fully aware that their son had absolutely zero self preservation skills, but weren't concerned enough about it to make any sort of a decision. Ray didn't possess, and didn't seriously desire to possess, the tools necessary for succeeding at college. It was as simple as that. Additionally, his parents conduct and attitude towards him began to create serious emotional problems for him.

Without my mom around, Ray got little, if any, support. Sure, he had a place to eat and sleep, but that was the extent of his parent's involvement. He was too much work for Brenda. Besides, she had been popping out babies one after another with her new husband and Ray didn't really even interest her. Ray did prefer to stay at her house but only because she didn't keep track of him at all, leaving him free to skip school with impunity and sneak out at night to get high, drunk and to prey on the cute, rich girls he was so enamored with.

For Kim's part, he seemed content to watch life kick Ray around and actually took joy in adding to the problem, though from his standpoint as a lifelong Okie, he probably thought he was doing Ray a favor. Kim had learned all he did about life on his own since his father, a raging and abusive alcoholic, served little if any function in his life and never had. What was good enough for Kim was good enough for Ray.

Several examples illustrate my point. My mom used to take all of the grandkids on a shopping trip for clothes each year in preparation for the new school year. Our sons always appreciated the gesture and went willingly, but were hesitant to take advantage of her generosity. They always got enough to satisfy grandma's desire to help out and little more. Ray, on the other hand, would take full advantage of the situation and would generally go home with over five hundred dollars worth of clothes. It was important to him that the clothes were all Tommy Hilfiger brand so everyone at school would think he was a person of means. He never figured out they mocked him for this, actually referring to him as "Tommy" behind his back.

When his grandmother died, so did the yearly shopping spree. Kim, recognizing the boy did need clothes from time to time, took him shopping one time, but rather than explain his monetary limitations to Ray, he let him actually try on a bunch of clothes and pile them up at the cashier in preparation for purchase. However, after all the time and effort, when it came time to pay, Kim told the salesperson he didn't ask for all those pieces of clothing and hadn't been consulted, even though he was standing right there, and refused to pay for them. I can only imagine how embarrassing it was to Ray to be smacked down in front of the salesperson, by your smiling dad to boot.

On another occasion, when Ray turned sixteen, he needed a means to get around. Kim took him out to find something and got Ray a type of motorcycle known as a crotch rocket, due to the fact is was capable of easily doing over 150 mph. Just the kind of thing an irresponsible sixteen-year-old needs for a first vehicle. Not only that, in order to get the bike, Kim forced Ray to get a bank note with steep monthly payments. When calculated, Ray would need to work at least thirty hours a week to keep up with payments and insurance. At the time, he was still in high school, skipping school constantly and doing poorly in his studies.

I didn't know what Kim was trying to accomplish with such an asinine move, but I did mention to Ray that he might want to see if his dad had recently insured him for a bunch of money because he clearly didn't care about his safety, much less his education. I also told Ray I personally thought it was a terrible move and that he would wreck it sooner than later, maybe at the cost of his own life.

It didn't take long. He actually wrecked it multiple times, eventually totaling it out trying to negotiate an interstate exit ramp with excessive speed where he and the bike snapped off a four by six inch post. After he quit crying and got out of the emergency room, he kept the post as a trophy of his exploits and was once again stuck without transportation.

When Kim eventually got remarried, he decided to leave Salina for greener pastures with his new bride, her own wayward kids, and their new child, but Ray wasn't welcome to come along. His dad told him there wasn't room in the new family for him, but he would do one last favor for him since Ray was his son. Kim had an old, practically worthless pickup and for only $1000, he would sell it to Ray. It didn't even run at the time. Ray wasn't that stupid and I'm sure he got the idea. Dad didn't want him around other than to take advantage of him. Kim seemed to think it all was a hoot.

Nothing changed during his senior year and Ray graduated with the class of 2003. He had grand plans, indeed. In the yearbook, he noted that he was going to Norway after high school, whatever that meant. He had dabbled in poetry, even plagiarizing several poems with great success. With the black turtle neck he had been sporting, maybe Norway would be his new inspiration. When I was asked, I told those interested maybe Ray meant the USS Norway.

His basic belief was that he would show up after high school and I, as the executor to his education trust, would simply dole out the cash. It didn't work out that way. I told Ray that I didn't believe he had what it took to succeed at college, but that it was possible for me to change my mind. Acting like a responsible person was my only requirement.

I really wasn't trying to be a jerk. I had for the better part of two years been trying to talk to him about this very subject, but it went in one ear and out the other every time. That behavior, in itself, was evidence of what I was alluding to. I was genuinely concerned with Ray's future and just blowing what little money was in his fund getting drunk and haunting girls didn't seem to be a prudent use of limited funds. My requirements were really quite simple. Acting like a responsible person for three months isn't an insurmountable obstacle for the rest of us. In retrospect, I really, really wish I had just given him the money and sent him on his way, out of our lives.

Chapter 4

When Ray spoke, it was like he was always laying the groundwork for something, though a person seldom knew what for. Recanting a strange story completely out of context was par for him. Every now and again, if you put all the disjointed stories together, not necessarily in the chronological order they were told, one could actually figure out what Ray was talking about, but it wasn't often. The reality was that Ray typically had so many lies and schemes working at once, it was impossible to remember it all and be able to weave a cohesive story together for everybody. The key was that people seldom compared stories.

Ray left Salina after graduation from high school and, with a friend, went to work for an uncle, one of Kim's brothers, in Arkansas. It's hard to tell what he did, but as near as can be determined, he partied the summer away, drinking beer and rafting, and earning money picking up construction materials on job sites. In mid-summer of 2003, Ray came up with a scheme typical of what I've been referring to. He had graduated from high school just a month or two before. Ray returned from Arkansas and came to visit me at work with an idea.

Ray and his buddy, Bret, had come up with an idea that would probably need some financing, hopefully from his college fund since it was, as he contended, an education in the real world. He produced two Polaroid photos that, when held side by side closely together, displayed a bed made of ropes. It was connected to the two walls that make up a ninety degree corner in a room. Sort of a triangular hammock supported on two of three sides by walls.

After apologizing for the poor quality of his visual presentation, he stated that they had come up with the idea one day and wanted to get some proper building materials to make one of the rope beds the way it should be done. Ray stated he was preparing to patent the design and had actually gathered up some written information from one of the other employees before I arrived at the office. Additionally, one of his uncle's friends had mentioned they might be able to sell the design to Walmart, whose headquarters were located just down the road from where he was staying in Arkansas

I hadn't mentioned a word up to this point and had just one question before he went on. Was he looking to set up a bed making business? I had known Ray for his whole life and was well aware that he seldom took reality into consideration in his grand plans, but his reply caught even me off guard. He wasn't wanting to set up a business. Ray just felt it was a shame to waste his talent gathered in five years of engineering and design work and wanted to showcase his talents.

Five years? He had just graduated high school maybe two months before. I asked him to clarify this point. He replied that he had, after all, taken a CAD class in school and worked as hired help in an automobile repair shop. To Ray, that translated to five years of study in engineering and design. I let him continue.

After spending the summer demonstrating his engineering and design skills, Ray stated their plan was to take their cash head off to Europe in the fall and possibly attend college. He seemed to be done presenting his plan so I began asking some pretty basic questions.

Where would he showcase his talents? In the middle of the yard, a storefront? How long would he promote his project before he deemed it a success or failure and headed off to Europe? Did he have any idea how much it costs to live in Europe? How much cash did he plan on taking? Did he have a passport? I informed him that Walmart didn't buy concepts, they bought things, usually by truckloads. Was he going to make a truckload of beds? The questions went on.

As I made my way through the list of what I thought were elemental inquiries, a look came over Ray's face. He became quite flustered, to the point that if smoke and sparks had come out of his ears, it wouldn't have surprised me one bit. He was sputtering, having lost the ability to finish a sentence and was beginning to turn red. I ended my round of questions with the big one. How much money do you want? Ray replied five hundred dollars.

I was momentarily dumbstruck. To accomplish what he was talking about would certainly take more than five hundred dollars and I had already prepared myself for a figure of ten times that. In my mind, it simply reinforced what I already knew. Once more, Ray was trying to scam me for money, for what reason was anyone's guess.

I ended the whole charade with a synopsis of the events from my perspective. What I was hearing was this. Both he and his buddy were tired of sleeping on the floor and one day, likely in a drunken state, they created a rope bed of sorts. Then one of his uncle's buddies, probably joking and half drunk as well, wandered by and told them they ought to market it to Walmart.

I told Ray patenting the idea probably wasn't an option since the design had been around as long as rope. I also noted that he better have a lot of money when he went to Europe because starving Americans on the street didn't garner much sympathy. Last but not least, I told him the simple fact that if two young men in the prime of their lives couldn't come up with five hundred dollars so they could chase their dream it was absolutely pathetic. I wouldn't have classified it as a more supportive moment between uncle and nephew.

When reality was at hand, Ray was always dense. His only question to me after my analysis of the situation was to inquire if that meant he wasn't getting the money. I affirmed that was the case. He thanked me, shook my hand and walked out the door, leaving the thick pile of information he had my staff work up for him relating to patenting and copyright law sitting on my desk. He didn't seem bothered in the least that I had basically stated I thought he was a liar, and a sadly lazy one at that. He certainly was resilient. You had to give him that.

However, a strange encounter the morning after his plea for cash did cause me some concern. It was before 7 a.m. I was standing in our backyard watering plants when Ray and Bret emerged out of the trees from the direction of the cemetery behind our house walking across the yard. Even though I was less than fifty feet away, they evidently didn't notice me until I startled them by yelling good morning at them. They jumped like a couple of rabbits.

Suddenly aware of my presence, they tried to regain their composure. Ray greeted me as they hurried toward the driveway and street, their pace dramatically hastened. Ray said they were just out for an early morning run and he decided he would bring his friend by our house to show him all of the wonderful improvements we had made. They walked off briskly and never once even glanced at the house, much less discussed it. Not once. His friend just stared straight ahead, conspicuously so. I stood there with my hose and watched them walk away, waiting to see Ray point out the changes. It never happened.

The whole premise of the encounter was beyond suspicious. Two unemployed eighteen year old young men got up at near dawn and while out jogging decided to cut across a cemetery and emerge into our backyard so they could check out the fabulous changes we had made to our house, but then forgot to look once they got there. It was probably beside the point that there were no improvements to look at other than a new coat of paint. All of this happened the day after I denied Ray money. I had little doubt they were attempting to case our house for a little robbery when I interrupted them. We discussed what happened as a family and Theresa and the boys were sure all the doors and windows were locked until Ray left town.

The next time I heard from Ray was when he called me near the end of the summer requesting money for school in Arkansas that fall. It was as though we had never spoken earlier in the year. It shouldn't have been a surprise when I said no. Once more, I attempted to explain what I required. He just didn't seem to get it.

He returned home to Salina at Thanksgiving and moved into his mom's house after his father and his new family relocated again, this time to Arkansas. Ray was told there wasn't room for him anymore and was asked to leave.

It's hard to tell what he did with his time once he returned home. He told anyone that would listen that he was in training for a marathon that would take place in the spring in Montana and he was planning on skydiving over the Rocky Mountains with fourteen of his closest friends. This all sounded strange, but if you knew Ray, everything he said was strange. Never mind that he was broke, had no vehicle, no job, no money, and was living with his mom. Questioning him just became confusing and frustrating, so nobody in the family did it anymore.

Ray spent late winter and early spring of 2004 training for his supposed exploits, though there weren't any set dates. He had begun spending his time with younger, actual students from the other high school in town, presumably because all of the people he knew from his days at his high school wanted nothing to do with him. He had used them up. Ray was basically out of sight until the first of March when his ways finally caught up with him, in a big way.

One of the younger kids Ray had been hanging out with since late fall of 2003 was Adam Bruna. He had met Adam at a local restaurant while briefly employed there. Ray had discovered in the six months since his graduation that real life was a pain, so reverting back to his senior year seemed a workable alternative. Adam was a gregarious, happy, and well liked young man, apparently willing to give Ray the benefit of the doubt or, more likely, didn't know his past at all. Whatever the reason, he couldn't possibly have known what he was getting into when he became involved with Ray Jones.

They both liked to spend time adventuring in the outdoors and having a good time. One evening in early March, Ray had what they considered a brilliant idea. They decided it would be quite an adventure to raft the raging Smoky Hill River and go over the usually ankle deep water falls. At the time, the shallow falls were more like six feet deep and were suggestive of what Armageddon likely resembles.

The Smoky Hill is generally a lazy, shallow river most times of the year, but springtime releases from the reservoir upstream had it running over fifty times normal rate with the water at a brisk thirty-eight degrees. Rafting the river was good fun on a hot summer day. I've done it myself on numerous occasions with friends and a six pack of beer. It would take over an hour to travel a mile and often our butts would drag on the bottom. The deepest part might have been six feet in some of the holes. Generally, a lot of time was spent paddling with hands to keep going. That's not how it was in early March though. With the state the river was in, traveling that same mile likely only took five minutes, if that.

The river was a terrifying sight to behold and the thought of even being near it, much less rafting it, was not something that came to mind in most observers minds. It reminded me of an angry blender. Not only that, the section they wanted to raft was located in a virtual canyon. The river had been rerouted years earlier, by digging a bypass basically, to prevent flooding in the city. This process took the new channel through a hill, thus the sides to the river were vertical for at least thirty feet, impossible to scale. The falls themselves, only six feet tall, wouldn't usually even qualify as water falls in most people's book. That week though, flowing at over 25,000 gallons per second and at over a quarter mile from our house, the bone jarring rumbling of the falls was clearly audible.

Ray and Adam, invincible in their youth, obviously didn't comprehend the gravity of what they were going to attempt. They initially tried to persuade others to accompany them but couldn't find any takers. Those that were present suggested they at least not attempt it at midnight, their original departure time. They agreed and waited until dawn. The itinerary change would ultimately save at least one of their lives.

Confidence must have run high. They didn't even wear life jackets, an incredibly idiotic act under any circumstances. In a newspaper article printed a year later, Ray stated that the anticipation was so great that they stayed up the whole night before waiting to launch at dawn. They spent the night playing disc golf by the light of the moon and playing a game called pog.

Not surprisingly, like others that had attempted the same feat over the years, things went predictably bad. They didn't even make it to the main falls. Ultimately, Ray was found screaming, clinging to a wood pile in the center of the river. Adam was gone, pulled under an adjacent wood pile by the torrential current.

It took several hours to rescue Ray, a testimony to the treacherous conditions faced by his saviors. A helicopter rescue was aborted and ultimately, an insanely brave member of search and rescue went into the water and drug Ray to shore. Other than some severe exhaustion and hypothermia, Ray was no worse for the wear. It took shutting the outflow gates at the reservoir and a couple of days before Adam's body could be located and retrieved.

One conversation at the time stands out in my mind and was a true testimonial to the state of affairs when it came to Ray. As mentioned, the section of the river where all this happened is quite close to the house we lived in at the time. That morning, as I was taking one of our sons, Ransom, to symphony practice, we passed all the commotion in the street. At the time, there were dozens of people and rescue vehicles on the scene and a helicopter hovering over the river. It was obvious to me a rescue was being attempted.

Ransom asked what seemed an innocent enough question. "What do you suppose is going on?" Without knowing anything other than what I was looking at as I drove past, I replied without skipping a beat, "Some idiot like your cousin Ray tried to go down the falls." Little did I know at the time that Ray was the actual focus of the rescue attempt going on. What happened was truly a tragedy, but not a surprise to those who had known Ray for any amount of time. It was a fact. He was dangerous to be around.

Chapter 5

The Allen boys were born in and brought up in Salina. Destry, born in 1986, was the oldest of the three boys. His brothers Ransom and Lucas were born in 1988 and 1991, respectively. Their existence was like something out of the 1950's, something that didn't just happen by accident.

Theresa and I are in our original and only marriage and for most of the boys' lives, both sets of grandparents lived less than a mile away. Theresa was a stay at home mom, a true homemaker. The boys did very well playing musical instruments, had good grades, were respected, conscientious and liked. They attended summer camps, fished, hunted, and golfed often. They had a cat and dogs, a big house and a big yard. We went on great vacations and the boys had plenty of spending money and cool stuff. Most significantly, they had unconditional support and love. All in all, the Allen boys wanted for nothing and, as a world traveler, I often reminded them of the fact. Ray, in contrast, had few of these things.

In spring 2004, Destry was very involved with his girlfriend, Nichole. He was also an accomplished trumpet player, church deacon, generally good student and loving son, but that spring, it was Nichole that really had his attention. They had been together for some time, but Theresa and I didn't know that much about her. Destry had stayed pretty quiet on the subject and asking questions of a teenager was like pulling teeth. She was sweet, polite and Destry loved her was all we really knew. He was an attentive guy, often following her home at night, since her car was unreliable.

He was growing up and at seventeen, over six feet four inches with red hair, looked even more grown up than he was. As with all seventeen-year-olds, it's impossible to know where they're at all the time. Put another way, are they where they said they were going to be, doing what they said they were going to do? Since it's not possible to monitor such things, a certain amount of trust has to be established, hopefully long before they want the car keys. Destry had proven himself to be trustworthy and responsible over the years and was trusted to run his life accordingly.

As a seventeen year old junior in high school, he was without doubt nearly a man. His, for lack of a better phrase, secret life with Nichole began to grow. It's not that we weren't aware to a certain degree and it wasn't extreme. Theresa and I both understood that in matters of the heart, some things have to be learned that parents can't teach. You hope they listen during the sex talk and the reminders you cleverly throw out later. Ultimately, sooner or later you just have to trust them.

I would be the last to portray Destry as an angel. For that matter, I've never met a kid that was an angel, though I've known a lot that wanted me to believe they were. Raising angels was never one of our parental goals. What Theresa and I hoped to accomplish as parents was to raise intelligent, thoughtful, worldly, grounded individuals that would eventually be great parents and productive members of world society. By our standards, Destry was already a more complete person than ninety-nine percent of the adults I know. He didn't really care if he was liked. We always told him the desire to be liked was a fundamental character flaw of humans and it was best not to waste any time cultivating it. What he desired was respect, and the two characteristics seldom go hand in hand.

One time when the school band was returning from a field trip to a nearby town, it appeared the bus accidentally left one of the band members behind. When the students on the bus discovered they had seemingly left someone behind, they laughed their butts off, except for Destry. He told the class they were all idiots. How would they like to come out of the building and find the bus gone? The instructor was informed of the situation and he was able to locate the student who, as it turned out, had gone home in a car with a relative. The move didn't raise Destry's popularity level with the crowd, but the teacher sure appreciated and respected him.

Had we known that Ray had reentered the picture as much as he had, we wouldn't have been quite so complacent. Before Adam died, Ray had been contacting Destry, trying to reestablish a relationship. Destry had matured to the point that he didn't mind being around Ray, as long as he kept watch on his wallet. He and Nichole didn't have a lot of friends so when Ray would call and suggest getting together, it didn't seem like such a bad idea. Ray had a girlfriend, Jessica McWhirt, so it was sort of a couples thing when they met. The only problem was that they gave Nichole the creeps.

So it came to be that when Ray and Adam prepared to make their fateful voyage down the river that night, Destry was one of the bystanders asked to participate that declined. Nichole later stated Destry thought the venture was insane, probably because he lived near the falls and knew what they were like. For whatever reason, Destry ended up with Adam's cell phone when he went home that night. It wasn't till noon the next day he realized he had a dead kid's phone in the back of his car.

Unfortunately, Theresa and I weren't made privy to this information until sometime after Destry's death by Nichole. I can understand Destry's hesitation to bring us into the loop. He knew we were down on Ray and his ways, and then the river accident happened. Lord knows what we would have to say, definitely nothing good. Besides, what had happened didn't seem to really have anything to do with his life, per se. It had just turned out that we were right after all about Ray, something we didn't necessarily need to be reminded of, again.

Though at the time of the river tragedy we were unaware of Destry's peripheral involvement, his interest from that point on did catch our attention. For the most part, we wrote it off as a natural fascination with a tragedy striking so close to home. He went to the hospital often over the days immediately following the accident in attempts to visit Ray. Presumably, the cell phone somehow got back to Adam's family.

Adam's funeral, like most for young victims of life's tragedies, was well attended. The story had been on the front of the local newspaper for several days and was well known to most. I wanted to support Destry and his desire to attend, but my disgust with Ray was so nauseating and visceral, I simply couldn't. Besides, I didn't even know Adam.

As far as I was concerned, the simple truth was the wrong kid died. I know that sounds harsh, but it demonstrated my state of mind at the time after a lifetime of Ray. It's always been my observation that people base a lot of stock in being right. I found being right about the simple truths regarding Ray after the fact didn't bring any satisfaction at all. In fact, it did the opposite. I couldn't even be around him anymore. Theresa decided to accompany Destry and Nichole. Their account of the funeral only reinforced my bitter feelings toward Ray.

Basically, as described to me by several eyewitnesses, he attempted to turn it into the Ray show. His emotional agony was so over the top that I was told by a member of the funeral home that never, in over several thousand funerals, had he witnessed such a performance. He told me he made a mental note to stay clear of Ray. Fellow mourners had to help Ray stand and walk. It didn't matter who you were. He'd grab hold and sob. Oh, what he had been through, the pain of it all. It was absolutely nauseating. He relished the attention.

Ray's performance, though creepy to many of the adults present, didn't really register with the kids. It probably resembled something they had seen on television, as if that mirrors reality. Truth be known, that's likely where Ray got the idea for his performance. One of the kids present said that immediately following a similar emotional outburst at the cemetery, Ray's only concern was for which limousine he should ride in.

Unfortunately, Destry bought the act. It was easy to feel bad for Ray. He seemed genuinely contrite and professed to a new interest in Jesus Christ. He took to constantly and conspicuously wearing a cross around his neck, framed by a red silk smoking jacket he had acquired at the Goodwill store. Most irritating, he wanted to shake everybody's hands.

Shaking hands isn't a bad thing, but like many social customs, there are certain unspoken rules which Ray didn't seem to grasp. He would shake your hand every single time he saw you, even if it was the third time that day. It was just weird.

Much like the funeral, Ray seemed to be trying to do what he thought was expected of him. He believed that adults shook hands, therefore as a new found adult he believed it necessary, to be convincing, to shake hands. My belief was that he hadn't changed an iota. He was just riding the pity train as long as it would keep him in the limelight and cash.

Destry, as the oldest and nearest in age of the Allen boys, was naturally closest with Ray. Whether we liked it or not, as generations of young men before him, Destry felt a certain loyalty to his older cousin. If nothing else, he certainly felt a bond. As a deacon at the church, Destry had been learning the virtues of giving support to those that need it. Ray, in his sadly pathetic state, seemed to qualify in Destry's mind as being in need of moral support, if nothing else. Ransom, Destry's brother, said Destry had even said as much to him.

Starting in April, Destry began to spend time with Ray and Jessie after midnight. According to Nichole, it was never more than once or twice a week and not necessarily every week, but it did become a new habit. One of the problems with having a full time girlfriend is that it can be isolating. Having Ray to spend a little time with when Nichole wasn't available was actually desirable to Destry, especially since Ray had seemingly turned over a new leaf after Adam's drowning.

Ray did come to one realization. He needed to address some basic problems with his game plan for life. For instance, it can be pretty difficult to keep a job without a vehicle, or get a job without clothes. Without a job, it's likely he wouldn't be able to eat much longer or, more importantly, as an investigation later would reveal, afford the illegal drugs he had developed an appetite for. Brenda, Ray's mom, had periodically booted Ray out of her house over the years, so even a roof over his head couldn't be taken for granted.

In the middle of April, he approached me seeking cash from his college fund to address these fundamental necessities. It sounded like he had a plan and though it wasn't what the fund was intended for, Ray decided to face the income tax consequences and buy the things that were needed. Besides, I couldn't very well keep his money from him when he was nearly starving, immobile, and homeless.

I found a good, used pickup for him and went with him to buy work boots, pants, and gloves. Old habits die hard though. In the course of the next month, Ray landed and lost at least three jobs. Cash flow was erratic so he was continually coming to see me, usually with girlfriend, Jessie, in tow. I gave him what he asked for – twenty five bucks here, fifty bucks there. I wasn't willing or desirous to get receipts as proof of his needs. At nineteen years old, Ray was a grown man, and it was his money.

His juggling act was in high gear in May of 2004. He needed money for gas, food and, especially, drugs. He needed to keep me happy, as best he could, without actually having to work. Jessie was his officially recognized girlfriend. Of course, that didn't stop him from having a sexual relationship with another girl, fifteen-years-old to boot, for most of the month, or leaving the state at one point to follow the new girl back home. He also mentioned a possible move to Lawrence was in the works and actually went there for a few days, then returned. When he was at his mother's house, he was always on the verge of getting kicked out, so he needed to keep Brenda happy as well. In the midst of all this, he was getting and losing jobs.

Plus, he had been pulled over in his truck while in Arkansas and jailed since he had never paid his DUI. Apparently, jails were full in Arkansas so they made a deal with him to pay so much per month for a prescribed period. His legal troubles with going over the falls were still also on the table. He had a backpack on the logjam when he was rescued that had marijuana, a pipe, and his wallet in it. Kids on the bank knew this even before he was rescued and their conversation regarding the issue was overheard by one of the many officers present. They retrieved the pack and found the stuff. Why Ray didn't get rid of it during the hours he sat there is anyone's guess.

Similarly, why he actually went to the police station and tried to claim it, resulting in his arrest, is anyone's guess. For whatever the case, they dropped the charges and let him off. Ray told me he wasn't smoking anything. He had just found the pipe and it was so neat he was going to frame it and put it on his wall. I didn't ask what the pot was for. What would be the point?

Ray's light was quickly fading. In fact, after having some time to think about it, many people had come to the conclusion that Ray wasn't exactly blameless in the river tragedy, even if he was lugging a big cross around his neck and telling everyone he had been changed by his experience. It was, after all, his raft that was used and until Adam met Ray, he hadn't been prone to do something so poorly thought out. Ray still didn't have a job and although he had his mom's roof over his head, he was right back to where he was before. No money, no vehicle and no phone. The new twist was that Destry, not Adam, was the new victim of his attention.

It was a tall order to keep track of all the details, especially when the details were made up as he went along. Even with all of his fancy maneuvering during the month, life was still catching up. His deceptions at his mom's house finally caught up with him and he was told to get out at the beginning of the week Destry died. It was a good thing he had his truck, because that was his new home. No others in the family were aware of this development at the time. There wasn't anyone left that would let him in their house. His one last chance at redemption was a bust. The poor kid who almost drown was back on everybody's shit list.

During the course of that May, it had slowly come to our attention through cell phone records and other clues that Destry was seeing Ray from time to time. Theresa was unabashed and direct when she told Destry, on at least three different occasions that month, that he would die if he was around Ray. After a lifetime of Ray's duplicity, deception, and thievery, and on the heels of Adam's death, she was no longer in the mood to mince words and didn't. Ray was a physical danger to anyone around him, period.

I'm sure it wasn't the first time a young man dismissed his mother's warnings as simply being paranoid and overprotective. I probably would have. Ray seemed OK and as long as he watched his butt around him, as he had learned to years ago, Destry probably felt it was a risk he could manage. After all, he didn't ever think the river fiasco was a good idea in the first place and refused to participate when asked.

I didn't keep track of Ray. He would come and go with Jessie, announcing why the most recent job didn't work out, his new plan, and hinting at cash needs. The second week of June found him without a job, again, and needing money, again. He was beginning to sound like a broken record. One day, in return for the money he desired, I required him to report to the church and help out on the grounds for the day. Even he couldn't think of a reason why he shouldn't do the work. By all accounts, he did more than he was asked, but not in a good way. That was the last encounter I remember with Ray before seeing him the morning I found Destry.

Chapter 6

Our pastor was standing outside when Ray wandered up to the house, around 12:30 p.m., the day I found Destry. He delivered the news to Ray of Destry's death during the night. Ray fell dramatically to the ground, floored by the news, and began sobbing uncontrollably. The scene was eerily reminiscent of his performance at Adam's funeral. Even the pastor didn't quite know what to do. After a minute, Ray pulled himself up off the ground and took his act inside, where a small crowd of people was located.

He hadn't stopped sobbing yet and parked himself on the sofa. One of Theresa's sisters noted Ray's arrival and demeanor. Tina, like all of Theresa's family, had learned not to trust Ray over the years. Keeping an eye on him was the norm. It wasn't long before he proclaimed to the heavens, between sobs, to anyone within listening distance, "Why does this keep happening to me?" Tina immediately told him to shut up. Nobody was in the mood for his bullshit. And that was that. He was suddenly totally in control.

Milling around grieving, like everyone else, wasn't what Ray had in mind. He craved the spotlight. In was pretty general knowledge, at least to the residents of the neighborhood, kids had been gathering at the spot on the river where the focus of the rescue and retrieval efforts had been after the ill fated river trip. A small cross was erected in memory of Adam. They weren't a problem as far as I know and the groups were never very large. Ray, and Destry we later found out, was one of the kids that would visit the site. The place was known as the curve, or Adam's Cross.

Standing in the kitchen, several of us were suddenly approached by Ray. Out of the blue, he volunteered the following. The night before, while hanging out at the curve, he saw Destry drive by. When I asked if there was anything else to it, Ray stated Destry waved and smiled real big, but Ray had no idea where he was going. I remember standing there thinking to myself that it seemed odd behavior for someone on their way to kill themselves. Why put on an act for Ray if you're so upset with the world that you've decided to shoot yourself? I wasn't sure what the part about not knowing where Destry was going had to do with it, but it was Ray's way to tell stories strangely and I left it alone.

And that was that. Ray quietly stole away. Nobody remembers him leaving. He didn't say goodbye to anyone or even offer condolences to either myself or Theresa. In fact, he never did. His act didn't work out quite the way he'd planned and, forced to improvise at the last minute to garner the attention he had to have, he spit out what he had to say and left. I watched him crossing the yard to his truck, struck by not only the lack of tears, but also by what seemed a cold smirk on his face. He didn't say much during his visit, but it was enough. "Why does this keep happening to me?"

Ray wasn't a part of the preparations over the next few days. In fact, we didn't want him around. He would just steal Destry's personal affects if not watched like a hawk. I told him directly to stay out of Destry's room. He certainly wasn't supportive in any useful way. Besides, to be honest, having Ray around, a person with seemingly no redeeming value, simply reminded us of the inequity of life. Two nice kids had died in the last three months, but Ray got to live. Where was the justice in that? For Theresa's part, just seeing Ray visibly upset her.

At the viewing of Destry's body for the family, Ray kept to himself in the back of the room. No one remembers him looking at the body or discussing anything. All in all, it was odd behavior. At Adam's funeral, a boy Ray only knew for a matter of months, he was inconsolable, constantly on the verge of a physical breakdown. At Adam's grave site, I was told he practically lay on the grave and pounded his fists. Yet the death of the cousin he had known since his first memories of life brought no tears, no physically debilitating sorrow. Never. Just quiet reflection. And one memorable incident.

At one point, it came to my father's attention that Ray was homeless, living in his truck, and the situation was common knowledge. The Allens, Ray's grandparents, worked hard all their lives in Salina to raise a family and were known to be vigorous, upstanding members of the community. His grandmother was known as a professional volunteer. Ray's homelessness, though of his own accord, was a poor reflection on everything Jim and Janice Allen had worked so hard to achieve, so my dad set out to find Ray and get the situation in hand.

It was during the days between the death and the memorial service. Everybody in the Allen clan was at our house that day, except for Ray. Ray's grandfather found him and Jessie at Brenda's, even though they were forbidden from being at her house for any reason, much less when she was away. The two of them had decided to take advantage of the opportunity for some sex in mom's house. Who cared if you weren't supposed to be there if you didn't get caught? It was classic Ray. He had by then discovered the grieving were the best ones to prey on, since their defenses were down in the first place. Or maybe screwing each other's brains out was just their own, personal way of grieving. I don't think his shocked grandfather thought so.

Chapter 7

After the memorial service, we tried to get on with life, as they say. We didn't believe it was a suicide, rather a horrible unexplained accident. There wasn't a note. Destry wasn't having suicidal ideations or even depressed. He even left out medication to take the next morning and all his lights on. In his phone call to Nichole at around 12:30 a.m. that night, he sounded fine. They didn't have any arguments. Yet within an hour, he decided to not only kill himself, but choose a method that was far from certain in its effectiveness.

Anecdotal evidence suggests that as many people live as die from a head wound caused by a .22 caliber round. He had shotguns and a large caliber rifle available to him if he wanted to do it right. It appeared Destry just got bored and killed himself on the spur of the moment with whatever he had on hand.

That type of mindset places a pretty low value on life and the repercussions of such a horrendous act. Destry had never been like that in his life. He especially loved family and holiday get-togethers. Every morning before school he would kiss his mother goodbye. The Allen house used the word love often. A desire to barely kill himself and force all of those who loved him to deal with the gory aftermath was the antithesis of his being.

Combined with my memory of no visible tattooing of the wound and the class ring, our belief was that if he had shot himself as the SO claimed, then it was an accident. The SO forced us to obtain a court order to gain access to the official report via our lawyer, which took some time. We waited and went through the motions of life.

Ray had been in and out of the Allen house for the week after the death, never with any predictability. The next week, we were scheduled to leave town to deliver Ransom, one of Destry's brothers, to a summer camp in upper Michigan. I decided to go out to the Depot, the first time since I had found Destry, to make sure the cleaning crew hired to handle the mess had done their job and locked up. I didn't really dread going out there. It just needed to be done. Life was supposed to go on was the theory.

At the last minute, I decided to take Ray with me, mostly because he grated on people. My sister, Jennifer, in town for the memorial service, had mentioned she felt obligated to have a heart to heart talk with Ray and try to get him to pull his head out. My judgment, from years of experience, was that she would have more success hitting her hand with a hammer. It was too late for him and I didn't want to spend another minute of family time in a fruitless effort. Survival seemed to be a more pressing matter at the moment. Getting him out of the house might spare everyone the all too familiar and useless exercise.

I don't remember what he said, but he talked non-stop all the way out to the Depot. I hadn't told him where we were going when we left home. At some point, I thought he might make some comment about our destination once he figured out where we were going. He never did. He just continued on with his inane jabbering, even as we pulled into the drive and proceeded to park in front of the structure. He didn't seem at all disturbed that we were visiting the scene of Destry's violent death. I just chalked it up to Ray's chronic weirdness.

As soon as we entered, a voice in my head, the same one as the day I had found Destry that told me not to touch the gun, demanded me to ask Ray if he knew anything about the night

Destry died. I really hadn't spoken with him since I'd found Destry. It had come to light in the last week that Ray and Destry were meeting intermittently after midnight. My intent when we left the house was to simply check on the place. Asking Ray anything never once occurred to me.

We were satisfied that Destry had a terrible accident and that was it. I don't know where my sudden inquisitiveness came from. I did what I was instructed too and asked him. Ray answered he knew nothing. For some reason, I decided to take it one step further. I told him that the truth would come out no matter what, that the SO had taken tire track impressions, dusted for fingerprints, collected DNA, etc. I'm not sure what I was getting at. I knew for a fact that they had done none of what I had just said.

By this point, we were sitting at the table Destry was sitting at when he was shot. I briefly recollected for Ray what the SO had told me, describing how it was believed Destry shot himself. I then revisited what he might know about the night, pointing out that the truth always comes out.

It occurred to me that I was asking about information that any normal family member would have brought forth already. In fact, it struck me that if Ray did have information about the night he hadn't already volunteered, maybe I didn't even want to know. I even said this, basically thinking out loud.

Having years experience in upper management participating in the corporate world, I never speak without thinking out where the conversation might be going. We were convinced that Destry had accidentally shot himself, maybe while taking off his ring. My suggestion that Ray might have information about the night he was withholding came as much as a surprise to me as him. I looked over at him.

At first, I thought Ray was in the infant moments of a seizure. His eyes were darting back and forth so quickly I felt sure he was going to hit the floor at any moment, flopping like a fish. That's not what happened though.

He leapt to his feet and screamed in my face, at the top of his lungs, "I DIDN'T MURDER YOUR SON!! I DIDN'T MURDER YOUR SON!! I DIDN'T MURDER YOUR SON!!!"

He ran out the door into the night, leaving me shocked and utterly stupefied sitting at the table. I got up and went to the door only to find him headed off down the road into the night on foot.

I walked out and asked him what the hell he was talking about. I had made no assertion that even remotely suggested he had done anything. Once again, as loudly as possible, he screamed "I DIDN'T MURDER YOUR SON!! I DIDN'T MURDER YOUR SON!!!", then ran full speed into the night. I began to yell for him to come back. I hadn't said anything about murder. As he disappeared into the dark, I reluctantly headed into the night trying to catch him.

I really couldn't have cared less if he wanted to run to the moon. My concern was more self serving. In the dark, he might fall into a dry creek that ran very close to the road and get badly hurt, or worse yet, hit his head on the concrete chunks in the creek used to control erosion. I remember thinking I didn't need this crap. My life was complicated enough with Destry's death. I didn't need any more problems, especially with my psychopath nephew. So I pursued him.

He didn't respond when I yelled for him to come back. I kept walking. It was incredibly dark. The Depot is located in the center of a square mile section, hidden deeply in the trees. The gravel driveway into the property is nearly a half mile long and nearest light is at least a half mile away, but not visible due to the dense tree growth. Though there was exterior lighting on the Depot itself, it wasn't on at the time, and was useless more than a hundred feet from the structure anyway. God, he was a pain.

I began yelling in the general direction of the road. "Destry's death wasn't your fault! It was a terrible accident!" I screamed this numerous times while I was stumbling along. Even in the heat of the moment, the thought came to me that the whole situation was getting surreal. I'm screaming at the top of my lungs into the thick of night, trying to communicate with some freaked out, totally unpredictable lunatic that I really didn't care about that much at the time, given my own problems. I was probably going to be the one that fell into the creek. It was at that moment I came upon him.

Ray was standing in the middle of the gravel road, about 300 feet from the Depot, sobbing into his hands. He looked so utterly pathetic I instinctively hugged him while he cried. We headed back down the dark road towards the Depot. After pulling himself together, his first comments to me were about how he had always been jealous of Destry and the fact that Destry had the type of family he wanted. He stated that he didn't have any family. He reiterated that he had always been so jealous of Destry. He even suggested that with Destry gone, maybe he could be more a part of our family, go on trips with us, maybe even move in. I just let him talk.

We reentered the Depot and sat back down for a couple of minutes. Since he seemed to actually be able and willing to discuss relevant life issues all of a sudden, I took advantage of the moment and suggested some things he needed to do. One of the questions I asked him will always stand out in my mind.

It was a pretty simple question, I thought. I asked Ray, "What do you think Destry would want you to do with your life?"

He pondered for a couple of moments and thoughtfully replied, "Have fun." I guess I just expected a little more from a guy that had lost his two best friends in the span of three months. I told him I thought that Destry would prefer he was productive.

We headed home, Ray in oddly high spirits, almost manic. He even volunteered a couple of heartwarming stories about Destry that happened during their exploits at night. They sounded like things Destry would have done and I would like to think they were true, but who knows. He was still Ray. When we arrived at the house, he walked in and announced to everyone that he wasn't the black sheep of the family anymore. He wanted to hug everyone. It seemed like a burden had been lifted from his shoulders. It was quite a moment.

As strange as all of this may sound, it's hard to overemphasize what a bizarre person Ray Jones is. After discussing it with Theresa, we both figured Ray was near the end of the very tentative grasp he had on sanity. I had always had a low tolerance for his shenanigans and he knew it. Maybe he just broke under the burden of my expectations. It was impossible to tell what he was thinking, so we quit trying.

Admittedly, our brains weren't working that well just a week after losing our oldest son, but we trusted the SO, as most people would. The professionals said he shot himself. True, at that point we disagreed on whether it was a suicide or an accident, but regardless of the semantics, both demises are by your own hand. The stretch from a self-inflicted death to homicide was unfathomable at that point, though I don't really know why exactly. Murdering yourself or being murdered would seem to be simply points on the same scale, but we found that's not how it works.

One other incident with Ray left us with the same confused, icky feeling. In the middle of July, on one of Ray's many visits, he sought out his Aunt Theresa reading a book quietly in the living room, a beautiful sunset out the full length picture windows. We had just returned from a journey to visit Ransom up in Michigan, back to back with a trip to Las Vegas. She was just relaxing, enjoying a book and glass of wine after a really long week.

Ray began by telling Theresa about what a great kid Destry was. He always wished he'd been like him. We must be great parents because Destry never complained about us. He reminisced about some vague warm and fuzzy memory involving Destry. Her reading interrupted, they went over and sat on the sofa.

He began again with a question for his aunt. Had she ever heard of "ice"? Ray mumbled something about meth. Theresa responded that yes, she knew what "ice" was. Anybody who's breathing knows about methamphetamine and the effects Kansas has experienced. Ray launched into a story about visiting his mother's house where, under the stairs in the basement, he had stored the drug in a box. It wasn't his, of course, he had been holding on to it for someone else since the river tragedy.

Recently, he had been partying, drinking hard liquor, and he had decided to do the "ice" he had found. He felt that this time, he would be able to control his emotions. But he was wrong. He lost control of his emotions again and did something so horrible to someone that he would regret it for the rest of his life.

He profusely reassured his aunt that he would never do anything like that again and wouldn't ever drink hard liquor again. Of course, he would still have a beer if someone were to come by his apartment, the one he had recently begun to occupy with Jessie.

Without missing a beat, Ray suggested that he wanted to do something for us. A counselor he had been seeing suggested he should repay our kindness. He thought making a dinner for us would be a good way to show his gratitude. Ray got up and left the room. He wasn't aware that I had eavesdropped on the conversation.

Theresa and I wondered what the hell he was talking about. Now what did he do? It had to have been a recent event since he referenced the river incident as having happened in the past. And what was it that we did, exactly, for him that he felt he should repay us. We had been politely shooing him away for the most part.

A few days later, Ray did follow through with a dinner, in a fashion anyway. We bought everything, fixed everything, and cleaned up everything, with the exception of the chicken breast strips that Ray charred on the brand new grill. It took nearly two hours to scrape clean later, when Ray wasn't around, of course. It was reminiscent of that occasion when you let your eight-year-old cook dinner. He seemed quite proud of himself

There were other oddities. In the weeks after Destry's death, Ray had been spending some time with Nichole and visiting her at work, a lumber yard, on regular occasions. These visits made Jessie intensely jealous. It seemed at first he was just trying to comfort her during a time of loss. As a cover to visit Nichole at work, he would buy some small, inexpensive part and then spend up to an hour talking to her at her cashier position. The behavior harkened of the obsessions he'd had with the girls in high school.

Upon closer examination though, all of his visits really centered around one thing. What did Destry and Nichole talk about during the phone call at 12:37 a.m.? Ray was so singular in his desire that Nichole finally told him not to ask about it anymore and in the end, told him nothing about the details of the call. When it came to our attention that he was hovering around her so much, we told her that she didn't have to patronize him on our account. She was glad to hear that since Ray had always creeped her out and she didn't like being around him. In fact, I finally gave Nichole a job where I worked so Ray wouldn't be able to bother her anymore.

We didn't see him much until the end of July. The reason for his visit, as with most of them, was a thinly veiled desire for more money. In fact, he had confided in Nichole the day before that if I would only give him his money, he would quit coming to our house. That was good, because I had absolutely no desire for him to continue coming to the house. His presence really upset Theresa. He was like Eddie Haskell gone really, really bad. I gave him several thousand dollars, made sure he understood the income tax ramifications of what he was doing, and sent him on his way. I was pretty sure we wouldn't be seeing him for quite awhile.

One other notable thing happened during that last visit. Ray was drinking V8 vegetable juice out of a can. He was always fascinated by our small fridge full of drinks and seldom missed a chance for a free pop or juice. As he was drinking the V8, he announced that he absolutely loved the stuff. I distinctly remember my first thought. That's interesting. An empty V8 can was found in the sink at the scene of the shooting. It had even been washed out.

We had always found it odd that Destry decided to clean the can before he presumably committed suicide. Pretty thoughtful for a kid about to make a mess that would take a hardened cleaning crew to put back in order. Whether it was Ray's can or not was irrelevant. What was relevant was the bell that went off in my head.

When he screamed "I didn't murder your son!!" in my face and professed to a deep seated, lifelong jealousy of Destry, nothing registered. When he confessed to have been drunk, high on speed, and lost control of his emotions, doing something so horrible to someone that he would regret it for the rest of his life, it went right over our heads. When he bugged Nichole for the details of their phone call before Destry died, about what he might have told her, it was just a weird curiosity. All of a sudden, an innocent can of V8 sparked a whole new awareness.

The report from the SO, via Tom, our attorney in Kansas City, arrived two weeks later. It was revealing, to say the least, in many different aspects. Exclusive of obvious official screw ups, the report raised more questions than it answered. One thing was crystal clear. Ray knew way more about the night than he had admitted to, basis his heretofore unrevealed phone call to Destry. All of a sudden, those disturbing experiences with Ray over the last two months made way more sense. We felt sick.

The strange encounters with Ray took on a whole new significance. Ray's bizarre psyche and the implications of his statements set aside, two things stood out. He didn't mention the cell phone call to Destry he made shortly before he was shot and Ray was also the first one to ever use the term murder in the same sentence as Destry's death.

A family friend, Jane, we spoke with about a week after getting the report expressed little doubt that Ray was involved. Her daughter, and her daughter's friends, had been stalked by Ray in high school. Jane was surprised that we didn't remember when, a year and a half earlier, she had warned us that she feared for the safety of our family.

During an apparent psychotic break, Ray showed up and walked straight into her house, without knocking, interrupting her cooking. He was unkempt, dirty, and his eyes were dark with a threatening demeanor. Having worked at a housing authority in a large metropolitan city when she was younger, Jane instinctively knew what she had to do to keep the situation from potentially escalating. She asked him into the living room, had him sit down, and asked him to tell her what was on his mind. Ray brought forth a poem he'd authored alluding to killing his mother. He hated her, he hated all Allens, especially me, and we should give him what he was due from his grandmother, who had truly loved him.

Shocked by what she was reading, Jane gathered herself and told Ray that killing his mother was the wrong thing to do. Jane felt strongly that she may have actually talked Ray out of killing his mom. As the conversation progressed, he suddenly realized she wasn't exactly the confidant he seemed to have convinced himself she was when he arrived, and just as suddenly got up and left.

Now that she mentioned it, Theresa did remember a conversation at a school PTO meeting from the previous spring of 2003. At the time, Theresa wasn't surprised by news that Ray was unstable and scary. What was surprising was that someone external of the immediate family had actually noticed. The information about his worrisome behavior, though new, was not out of character for the Ray Jones we knew. Theresa filed it away in her mind in the bulging weird-things-about-Ray file. But that was before Destry was found shot dead.

Chapter 8

When I saw the blue Ford pickup headed up the driveway, I found myself with my stomach in my throat. Though many scenarios anticipating this moment had come to mind in the last couple of weeks, this hadn't been one of them. For some reason I had a strange belief that the situation would be much more in control than it appeared it was going to be. Why I had any expectation there would be an element of control is comical in retrospect.

It had been several weeks since my nephew, Ray Jones, had been to our house. In the first two months after Destry's death, he had become a regular at our home, visiting on over twenty occasions. He never really had a reason for coming over, other that the obvious – to get money. Why he needed the money was anyone's guess, literally. The truth and Ray Jones were strangers and had been since he was a child. It was known by all that were acquainted with Ray that the only reason to ask him for an accounting of his expenses, or anything else for that matter, was to hear creative deception at its best.

Generally, his visits were intended to feign interest in the family, but somehow always ended in his desire to take some possession of Destry's or get some more money out of an account intended for his college education. The thought of Ray heading off to college was becoming more remote by the day, whereas the prospect of simply feeding and clothing him had become a real concern. Working, as with the truth, was something Ray didn't like to worry himself with.

From my perspective, for whatever the reason, it was obvious Ray needed to eat. Forcing him to figure it out for himself would simply result in him taking advantage of some unsuspecting acquaintance as it had for months, though in truth, there were few left to con. More likely it would result in missing items from our house, as had often been the case over the years. Letting him waste his own money seemed to be the least destructive option.

Having said that, I was tired of his duplicity and pesky visitations and, finally, at the beginning of August of 2004, I gave him more cash than I had been in previous visits, hoping to keep him away for awhile. His presence generally caused a nauseating discontent, was bothersome and his disputable concern about our family grated on everyone. Ray never did anything unless he wanted something. It had always been that way. One couldn't do anything about it, but since Destry's death, nobody was in the mood to patronize him anymore.

It seemingly worked until the eighth of September. As I saw his truck flying up toward the house that day, it seemed most likely that he simply needed another cash infusion, even though he had managed to get and, more importantly, keep a job for the last few weeks. That was a new twist. Of course, he might be coming over for a different reason, the one causing the knots in my stomach.

We had been spreading the word over the last couple of weeks that Ray was somehow involved in Destry's death, information that had come to light when we were finally able to get our hands on the official SO report. Ray, Destry's cousin, spoke with Destry by phone shortly before his death, one of many details the SO neglected to mention to us. More significantly, Ray had neglected to mention it in all of his visits over the last three months.

Destry's unexplained death at the beginning of the summer had shattered the lives of countless people that shared his life. Indeed, we were concerned with Ray and what he knew, but our more immediate concern was to let everyone know that it wasn't the simple suicide initially presented. That the faith they had in Destry likely hadn't been betrayed by his supposed last, selfish actions. Saving the sanity of those we cared about was the real goal of our information campaign.

It had always been likely Ray would eventually hear about what we were alleging, but since his reaction, like everything he did, would be unpredictable at best, I didn't spend a lot of time worrying about it. I guess I just assumed we would be the ones to initiate any conversation that was going to take place. As a hard and fast rule, Ray detested responsibility and the truth, so I didn't really think he would want to purposefully put himself into a position to address his lack of those particular virtues. Watching his pickup tear up the driveway that day, it occurred to me that maybe I should have spent a little more time pondering the possibility.

Chapter 9

After I noticed Ray driving up toward the house, I went to the kitchen to get a glass of ice tea and told Theresa of his arrival. He walked in without knocking. Ray never knocked anywhere he went and it didn't matter how well he knew the occupant. I was adding ice to my drink as he appeared in the kitchen. He didn't look well. He was pale, short of breath, and had a somber look on his face. A bit like a bad hangover and he was going to throw up any minute.

I said hello and asked him how the new job was going. He worked part-time hours on an early morning shift and got off late mornings. He still had on his company shirt. The month before, Ray had stated that his employer saw great potential in him and was looking at transferring him to the northwest region. I thought it was a load of crap. Nonetheless, attempting to make light conversation and catch my breath, I asked him if he had heard anything more in regard to his possible transfer.

As I made my way to the living room, trying to figure out how I was going to handle the situation, Ray mumbled something about how everything was going alright. He seemed distracted, something else on his mind. As I sat down on the sofa, he stood in the doorway to the kitchen, a distance of about twenty-five feet separating us. My only thought was that since he was the one that sought me out, I would let him do the talking and try to limit my part of the conversation to lawyerly, elusive responses. I knew two things for sure. I wanted information and he would run if I got to direct in my interrogation of him.

The impetus for his visit, we determined later, wasn't that he had heard we had found out about the phone call to Destry. He knew that before September 8. Ray sought us out because he found out from Nichole that not only did we know there was a phone call, we knew it was over four minutes in duration. Even he, out of touch with reality most of the time, realized not mentioning the call was incredibly suspicious. He needed to do some damage control.

According to Nichole, the fact that she knew this detail visibly caught him off guard. He had just gone to great lengths to describe to her how short and uneventful the call was, about how Destry was already at home when he had called him, but was tired and wanted to go to bed. Already at home? Why would he say that? She replied that they must have talked about more than what he claimed, since the call was over four minutes long. All of a sudden, I'm sure Ray wondered what else we knew, or for that matter, what else did everybody know? He immediately headed for our house.

Leaning in the door frame, he got right to the point. Recently a friend of his that lived in Kansas City had contacted him. She'd heard that Ray had killed himself because he was involved in Destry's death. He wanted to know if we knew why people would say such a thing. It was substantially the same thing he had told Nichole earlier.

I replied that was quite a story, but he knew how people are. Always talking about things they don't know anything about. Ray went right on. Though I hadn't asked, he felt compelled to recount for benefit of my memory how he had told me everything he knew about that night. How he had seen Destry drive by and how they waved at each other, though he didn't know where he was going. He hastily added how they had talked on the phone to each other and how he had come over the next day. I replied sure, I remembered all of that. He went on briefly about a couple of other irrelevant points. It was then I stopped him as though something had just occurred to me.

I asked him to go back a minute. Sure, I remembered his recollection of waving at Destry, but I didn't remember his talking about a phone call. Ray stated, oh yeah, he had brought that up. He had told several others. I stated, as a fact, that he hadn't told anyone, He hadn't mentioned it to me, period. He asked if I was sure. I told him I was pretty sure I would remember if someone related to me the last conversation my son would ever have.

"Oh, my mistake" was his response. Mistake? What was his mistake? Not telling us? His memory? His assumption we would never find out about it? He had just stated with certainty that he had told several people about the call, not just me. Was it his mistake that in each and every separate instance, he mistakenly remembered telling others something he didn't actually tell them?

The way he said it was an entirely different matter. You'd of thought I'd just pointed out that he forgot to pick up a gallon of milk on the way home from work. He acted as though simply saying that it was his mistake, whatever that meant, was the end of it. I didn't mention any of my thoughts.

For purposes of the conversation, I moved on with what I thought would be a natural response, now that the mistake had been cleared up. I asked him what in the world they had talked about. I'm sure it occurred to even him that my demeanor was strangely calm and friendly, considering the subject matter. He stated he and Destry had talked about some little stuff, but Destry was really tired and was going to head home to go to bed. Most interestingly, he claimed he didn't know where Destry was calling from. That was different than what he had told Nichole. Ray told her that Destry called from home, already getting to bed. I didn't even bring up the length of the call.

Four minutes is a long time in terms of conversation and he had only accounted for about twenty seconds. Since he had just come from talking to Nichole, he would have known that I knew about the length, after all, that's what brought him to the house. Yet I wasn't mentioning it, not like me at all. When it came to him, I was always about the details. That's why dealing with me was always problematic and required forethought on his part. The rope bed was a perfect example. He must have thought it was important to find out what was known to put himself in such a dangerous position on purpose.

In other words, he knew I was up to something. It might sound odd, but I was getting a certain pleasure out of playing a player, lying to the liar. As a rule, they always assume they're the only ones with a devious agenda. They prey on the honest nearly all of the time and get lulled into a certain comfort zone. Most times, it never occurs to them that others can play the game too.

He got back to his real concern. Did we think he was involved in Destry's death? I stated that there were a lot of questions that needed to be answered but one thing was for sure. Destry wasn't alone when he was shot. I replied I didn't really have any thoughts one way or the other until the investigation was complete.

Ray suddenly volunteered that he had been at the Depot with Destry about two weeks before his death, so if his fingerprints were found there, that was why. I asked him what they did during the visit. He stated that Destry took him over to the side of an old garage and showed him the area we used for target shooting, so that was why his footprints would be found over there. Then they went into the Depot where Destry pointed out a glue board used to trap rodents.

Both the Depot, and the caboose located in front of it, were moved to the site by a Salina doctor and his wife in the late 1970's. Without knowledge of the Depot, Ray's description might not sound as strange as it really was. The building is a circa 1880's Santa Fe rail depot, moved from its original location in Canton, Kansas, a small town about thirty miles south of Salina. It was converted to a country home, sitting on a site completely buried in trees in the center of a square mile section of land. The gravel road begins in a wheat field and meanders into a tunnel of trees encircled by the creek.

The Depot is one large room twenty by forty feet, with a partial open bedroom loft at the end, a room and bathroom located under it. It's a tall building, sidewalls thirteen feet with rough, open trusses. The apex of the peak is nearly nineteen feet off the floor. It has since been remodeled, but at the time of the shooting, there was also a small, single room added on which served as a hot tub room.

As mentioned, there is also a 1905 Rock Island caboose sitting on short rails right in front of the Depot. When decommissioned, the caboose was brought to Salina by rail, loaded onto flatbed trailers and trucked to the site. The Depot has another name tied to the whole move – Enadaline Station.

An old, southern railroad man helped with the set-up and when it was finally complete, wiped his forehead and declared, "Dat sho' nuf is da en' a da line fo' dat ole' caboose." The End of the Line, or Enadaline, Station. The doctor's wife immediately fell in love with the name.

Most people, when visiting for the first time, are completely enamored with the old caboose, the history of the Depot or the fact the residence, though technically on the plains, is deep in the woods only a mile from town. It's an unusual place by Salina standards.

Apparently not for Ray. He never even mentioned seeing a caboose on his first visit. What he remembered were bullet holes and mouse traps. Obviously, I needed to check out the target area. Later, I did look. I found a new target and bullet holes.

I continued with the interview. How did he like the Depot? Pretty cool, huh? Did he see the room out back? And how about the bathroom and shower? Last, but not least, had he gone up into the loft and checked out the view of the room? He replied he had.

This last question was the only one I cared about and what I had been working toward with my other questions. The .22 caliber pistol that was kept in the Depot was stored on top of a kitchen cabinet. From floor level, it's out of sight, but if you're up in the loft, a person wouldn't be able to miss seeing it. In other words, by Ray's own admission, he would have known where the gun was.

Ray began to take over the questioning. Didn't they find Destry's fingerprints on the gun? What was causing the belief that Destry wasn't alone? Without knowing one way or another, I replied that no, Destry's prints weren't on the gun. Ray was flabbergasted by the revelation. Besides, I told him, everyone knew how to put a gun in someone's hand, so it wouldn't matter if his prints were on it or not. I also told him that empty casings were found on the scene, a true statement. He instantly asked where at. I replied I couldn't really share that information with him. All that we really knew was Destry wasn't alone.

Why he was so interested in the details was the real question. What did he care about fingerprints on a gun, or the placement of spent casings at the scene? My desire was to give him disinformation and see what he did with it. If he was at the scene, he would know it was wrong, or it would at least give him pause to consider that he had missed something in the haste of the moment that night.

In response to my information, the look on his face seemed to say it all. He was in disbelief. It wasn't my assertion that someone else was present when Destry was shot that drew this reaction. My impression was that he was positive Destry's prints would be found on the gun and that he didn't remember any spent casings.

Somewhere along the line, he informed me that Jessie was with him all night the evening in question, so he had an alibi. This was the first time I had ever heard her name brought up in reference to the night. Ray had never said he was alone at Adam's Cross, but he had also never said anyone was with him. Interestingly, it had occurred to him before he came to our house that he would need to have an alibi for the night. He ended the alibi story with a suggestion that Nichole might somehow be responsible.

In fact, Jessie had completely disappeared from the scene as far as our house was concerned. She came with Ray on a regular basis before Destry's death, but hadn't been at the house a single time with Ray since. I informed him, without any factual basis I might add, her word wouldn't really matter. Prosecutors would likely dismiss her testimony. This one statement from me planted a seed of doubt that would later cause Ray to make a mistake.

The conversation kept going back to whether we thought he was involved and, more pointedly, did we think he had shot Destry. My pat answer was that I didn't have any belief one way or another and was waiting for the results of the investigation. For the record, I knew there was no investigation, but Ray didn't need to know that.

Our conversation went back and forth. At that point, I had gathered enough from his own statements to begin carefully working them back against him. For instance, ask him why he thought forgetting to tell us about the call wasn't a big deal? By then, I had gotten my feet under me and was preparing to dissect him. That was until Theresa came into the room.

She had been sitting in the next room at a computer listening to my patient, gentle interrogation and couldn't take it anymore. I had spent a lot of time in the presence of lawyers in my professional life so I knew well how to play the game. I was relishing my position in the conversation, but the process took time.

I think most people, believing the person in the next room was responsible for the death of their child, likely would have responded as Theresa did. She had lost her patience with me and my plan and was more than happy to answer his inquiries. Theresa approached Ray from the kitchen. He turned toward her and confronted her point blank. Did she think he had something to do with Destry's death?

I was sitting in Theresa's visual sight line, a little behind Ray, making an exaggerated slashing motion across my throat, repeatedly. Translation: "Shut up! Please, stop! I'm begging!" But there was no stopping her. How do you stop a mother from confronting a person, someone she helped raise, someone she took over three hundred photos of, about killing her son?

Theresa told Ray somewhat diplomatically, but without hesitation, that there were only two people Destry had been seeing at night, him and Nichole, and Nichole didn't do it. Well, that was that. Ray's eyes went dark, his face contorted, and he rapidly headed for the door. He ran and jumped into his truck and sped off. I didn't attempt to stop or follow him.

I knew up front he would run if cornered, just like all the other times in his life. The reaction was so predictable that I had actually planned to have friends put his truck up on blocks when he visited. Then it occurred to me that he might have a weapon with him and the plan was abandoned. Besides, what would I do with his truck?

I was furious with Theresa, but I couldn't really blame her. Parents aren't supposed to have to interview their child's potential killer. I'm told that's what competent, professional law enforcement is for. Unfortunately, we don't have that in Salina.

In retrospect, I have to ask myself, what kind of person had I become that could sit in the room with a person I believed shot and killed my first born son and have the emotional wherewithal to dispassionately dissect his story. Truth be known, I was beginning to enjoy myself. However, if I had to do it over again, I'd do it different. No clever games, just him on his knees with a shotgun in his mouth and some very pointed questions.

That was the last time we saw Ray without a lawyer being involved. He was the wronged party and we were simply terrible people. He just couldn't bear to be around anyone in his family that believed such awful things about him. Oh, the pain. It hurt so badly. How could we be so mean? He'd given what answers he was going to and we were just being spiteful. He didn't have to put up with that. It wasn't his fault we couldn't remember what he hadn't told us.

Chapter 10

I taped a letter to the windshield of Ray's truck a couple of days after the visit on September 8 pointing out significant problems with his story. I knew he wouldn't open the door to me. I asked too many questions and just confounded him. In the initial instance, a case could be made for Ray that since he wasn't even questioned, he just simply forgot to mention it, much as a child wouldn't mention his role in breaking a vase unless asked. We were operating on the premise that now the information about the night was coming out and we were asking, he would hopefully confess to whatever his role was. Destry wasn't just some stranger. He was Ray's cousin and friend. Surely the boy had at least a semblance of a conscience. Let that be a lesson in making assumptions. Narcissistic sociopaths don't have consciences.

The letter also suggested he should come forward and take care of this problem like a man because it wasn't going away. Running wasn't going to help. I suggested he go to the authorities with someone he felt comfortable with and get his story out. Heck, accidents happen, but by not talking about it, it made it look less like an accident. Not surprisingly, he didn't find any of my observations or suggestions helpful and holed up in the apartment.

Our initial viewing of the SO report and photos did one thing. It was obvious that someone with more acknowledged expertise than I had should look at the photos. Our attorney in Kansas City had gotten the reports for us, but his field of expertise wasn't criminal law, so initially I took them and the photos to our attorney in Salina, Julie, for her analysis. She had served as the Salina County prosecutor for a number of years. She, in turn, got together with Darrell Wilson, a past Saline County Sheriff, to get his opinion on the case. While they were doing all this, I studied the photos more myself in an effort to find additional clues that weren't so obvious at first glance. What I was really doing, I suppose, was trying to find a way to make the scene make sense.

We decided to conduct enough of an investigation to at least convince the SO, when we approached them, that it wasn't all our imagination. This seemed important because no matter how you cut it, we would be telling them they hadn't done their job. Tom had found a highly reputable and credentialed forensic pathologist that was hired to analyze the photos of the scene, about the only evidence that wasn't destroyed by the SO. His curriculum vitae included teaching at the University of Missouri and working with Homeland Security. I included a statement of my personal observations. A private detective was also engaged, a retired FBI agent, to conduct specific interviews and acquire cell phone records.

For my part, the time spent pouring over the photos of the gory aftermath of what had been our son paid off. The scene had never been reconstructed. It was clear from the photos that the SO moved the table to access Destry's body. One indication was they hadn't put the table back where it had been originally or the chairs. Setting the table back in place was relatively simple. The chairs required a little more thought.

One thing occurred to me. If the cleaning crew hadn't cleaned the chairs, the mixed fluid spatter on the legs would indicate the positioning. One of the nuances the killer attended to, in an effort to obscure the fact that Destry had been moved from where he originally fell, was to take Destry's arm, fully extended, and sweep it back and forth.

Destry had been found front down, lying in a straight line, legs together and his head facing to the right. This sweeping motion, quite forceful, spread vomit, blood, and cerebral fluids out in a fan type of pattern from his face toward his feet. Since we believed he was placed under the table, that meant the spatter had to cover the legs of the table and chairs that surrounded him. There were several different types of chairs, but there were four, all matching, of primary interest.

The one Destry had supposedly been sitting in was to his left at head height and on the opposite side of the fluids, which were to Destry's right, the side he was facing. Logically, there shouldn't have been anything on that one, as with the one at the other end of the table. One of the chairs had been beside Destry, on his right at about knee level, and the other at his feet. Again, logically the one on his right, sideways to him, the closest and in the direct path of the spatter, would have its legs covered all on the same side. The one at his feet, facing his feet, and further away, would have less spatter and what there was would be on the front of the legs.

Sure enough, the chairs hadn't been cleaned. After I caught my breath at discovering the remnants of my son's bodily fluids, I checked each chair and it was just as I had theorized. Two had nothing, one had a lot of spatter on the same sides of all four legs, and the last one had a little bit on the fronts of the legs. I put them all back in their original places basis my revelations. The exercise had been satisfying but hadn't actually accomplished anything.

As I was sitting there drinking a beer pondering the situation, I noticed something on the chair that had been on the right of Destry's body, at knee level. On the top of the chair, on the backrest, was blood spatter. Pure blood spatter not mixed like the floor, and not only that. The directionality of the drops indicated the blood was coming from the wrong direction, not from where Destry was sitting, unless Destry had boomeranging blood. By any investigatory standards, this was a significant find.

Am I an expert in blood spatter? Of course not, but by the same token, I'm not an imbecile. It doesn't take an immense amount of knowledge to know that blood can't go through metal or that it can't reverse its path of flight in mid-air. What I was looking at was what is known as a cast off blood pattern, likely made by the killer unconsciously shaking the blood off their hand. It appeared that after setting up the scene on the table the way it was *supposed* to look, all the while standing at the end of the table over the chair, the killer shook his hand resulting in the blood droplets.

I took the chair home and the next day, called Julie and asked her to find a blood spatter expert for me. She said she would. Next she asked who from the prosecutor's office had come to the scene the day Destry was found? I responded none had. She stated I had to be mistaken. When she ran the office, all serious crime scenes were visited. That was the policy. It was also official SO policy to notify the prosecutor's office. Once again I responded that no one had come from the prosecutor's office. My dad was at the scene the whole time until the cops locked the door and gave the key back to him.

For a second, there was a silence from her end. Julie stated she would get back in touch with me about the spatter expert. I tried to call numerous times and left messages over the next several weeks to no avail and went to pick up the whole file to give to our attorney, Tom, in K.C.

Knowing what I know now, I wouldn't have touched our case with a ten foot pole if I were her. I was happy Julie had done as much as she had. She had to live in Salina with her family. Not only that, she wasn't a prosecutor anymore. She was a defense attorney and, as such, I'm sure she had to be careful of the appearance of going after people similar to the ones she defended on a frequent basis. I know that would have occurred to me if I were her.

Plus this fact. We, meaning her and the Allens, went after the county prosecutor and police chief, then Destry, her client, was found dead, shot nearly between the eyes. The people that we were suing, who, by coincidence, happened to be in charge of finding your client's killer, didn't do their jobs and the killer happened to get away. It all had ominous overtones.

As I was preparing the report to go to K.C., I noticed a hand written note from retired Sheriff Wilson. Most of it was formulaic questions he came up with while reading and observing the report and photos. However, at the end of it, he notes that the more he looked at the photos, the more things didn't make sense and the more questions he had. One of his last comments states that it's "a funny looking suicide if you ask me..." I couldn't have put it better myself.

Late in November, I heard from Tom. He had a very serious tone and, since I was driving at the time, insisted I pull over and park so we could talk. The forensic pathologist had finished his examination of the photos and noted five distinctly separate indications of a homicide. He was positive about his conclusion. The doctor didn't even know about the screen door at the front of the building, broken, torn from its hinges and the fabric ripped, nor the chair with the blood spatter. Certainly, most people would have to include those additional tidbits as clues it wasn't a slam dunk suicide.

The information didn't shock me as much as our attorney probably thought it would. It simply affirmed what we had already figured out for ourselves. However, the sickening details were even more disturbing than I could have imagined.

In short, Destry had been shot from several feet away, his body moved and repositioned in an amateurish attempt to simulate a suicide. This was known because the bullet had partially fragmented and spread out slightly before it struck him, something that's impossible if the gun is fired point blank, tight against the skin. Based on the soot ring that he also observed, the doctor agreed the weapon was put to Destry's head after the shot, not before it. The table top with the blood, gun and photo was set up in entirety.

This wasn't a simple shooting. The killer chose to put in some grisly, up close and in your face effort. It would have been hard to keep from getting bloody. Plus, Destry was still alive during all of this, gurgling and bleeding everywhere, at one point vomiting. On top of that, if it was Ray, he knew his victim like a brother.

It seemed we were getting enough information gathered to present a cohesive argument to the SO. Everything seemed like it was falling into place. One thing we spent time considering was whether the case should be presented by an out of town attorney versus local counsel. There is a perception in Salina that bringing in hired guns from out of town doesn't play well with the powers that be. True or not, that's what we were working through. We finally decided to use a local, civil attorney that presumably hadn't ruffled any feathers on the criminal side of the system.

Meanwhile, my father, Jim, was getting remarried late in November. Ray was asked not to attend due to the unrest his presence would cause since nothing had been resolved. It was a big family event. One of the guests was a cousin that worked as an investigator for a sheriff's department in a nearby county. We hadn't seen any extended members of the family since Destry's funeral. Understandably, it had been an awkward occasion with little conversation.

While standing around at the reception, John told Theresa again how sorry he was about Destry and hesitantly mentioned that he heard there was a note. Theresa was perplexed. What was he talking about? There was no note. In detail, he stated how he had called the SO the day Destry was found and spoke with the officer in charge of the investigation. When John expressed concern that it seemed out of character for Destry and began to press for details, he was abruptly told Destry had left a suicide note. Suicide notes are many times used as definitive proof since they're often hand written and may actually cite a reason for the act. My cousin accepted what he was being told at face value and thanked them for their time.

Theresa reiterated. There was no note. None. In fact, the only instruction they gave us the last time we saw them was to let them know if we found one. John turned bright red and became visibly distressed. As an investigator, he was used to low life scum lying to him all day long. Evidently, cops' lying to him was a whole different, infuriating matter. We filled him in on what our investigation had uncovered so far.

This new information was truly disturbing. Not only had the SO not done their jobs, they actively discouraged anyone else from looking into the death either. No wonder they didn't want us to have possession of their half assed report. Talking with the Saline County officials was looking more adversarial by the moment.

John's involvement in the case especially aggravated the situation since he insisted on taking our reports straight to the Child Death Review Board and KBI. In other words, by the time we spoke with Saline County, the higher ups at state level would already know about their problem and would have been told to expect a call from Saline County. KBI can't get involved unless asked. I couldn't have cared less if John's actions pissed them off. I was beginning to get real pissed off myself.

One other detail compounded things. We, on behalf of Destry, were in the process of suing Saline County for one million dollars for liable and malicious prosecution of Destry at the time of his death. Two weeks before he was shot, our attorney had notified Saline County of a lawsuit related to the conduct of the county prosecutor, Ellen Mitchell, and the Salina Police Chief, Jim Hill. Destry's death killed the lawsuit. Coincidentally, it would seem, Destry's demise had saved them from what would have been a potentially career ending, very public airing of their lack of respect for the law, the constitution, and the citizens of Saline County.

Chapter 11

In the fall of 2002, Destry had a run in with the Salina Police Department (SPD). If you're a teenager in Salina, it's difficult to get through high school without SPD eventually coming after you. It's their one true specialty and everyone knows it. An attorney that works intimately with the city even admitted to me that he knew city leaders were aware of this conduct but just turned their heads. The targeting provides a nice living for the community's various defense attorneys.

The game works like this. They accuse you of some crime and you're expected to pay the fine, court costs, etc., or you can hire an attorney, go through endless continuances, and beat it in court. Of course, it costs a whole bunch more to actually pursue justice and the cops and the prosecutor know it. Though the accused want justice, most can't afford it. It's called a shakedown in layman's language.

That what they tried to do to Destry, to the point of prosecuting him for a crime that someone had already been convicted of. Not only did Destry not commit the crime, I personally had to find the actual perpetrator and convince him to confess, which he did. He was convicted. One would think that would be the end of it, but that was actually just the beginning.

One night in late October of 2002, someone drove through a newly planted yard landing in a new neighborhood in east Salina. Destry, already sixteen, had spent the night with a couple of friends. Late at night, they snuck out and drove around for the rest of the night in Destry's vehicle, a green Ford Explorer. Early the next morning, they were pulled over by SPD and accused of driving through the yard which was a few blocks away.

Destry was followed home by Officer Staley. He stated that Destry's green Ford Explorer had driven through the yard, the tire tracks matched, and they had an eyewitness. I was more amused than anything. I asked him if he had any idea of how many green Explorers there were. He pointed out the tires matched the tracks. Staley also pointed to muddy gravel on the Explorer. I asked him if the home owners had planted their yard on a gravel road and he responded that Destry had later driven through a vacant lot that was, presumably, muddy gravel.

Whatever. As far as crimes go, it wasn't much. I took him at his word since he was a law enforcement professional. It wasn't until later when I went to look at the tire tracks for myself that I realized Officer Staley was either blatantly lying or so blind to render him utterly useless as a professional whose livelihood is dependent on skills of observation. More of interest was the fact that a vehicle, the same vehicle judging by the tracks, had evidently driven through the same yard the night before Destry was accused. There were two distinct, separate tracks.

Anticipating rain that night, I later went over to the scene in the dark with a camera to document the actual tracks. Make no mistake. I was mad. The owner of the house awoke and noticed my car lights and activity. I apologized and explained what I was doing, probably just confusing and scaring her more than anything.

First thing in the morning, I went over to take more photos, even though it had, indeed, rained during the night. The tracks were obscured and mostly useless, but as I was looking, Officer Staley pulled up. He was responding to a call by the resident from eight hours before in regards to someone taking photos in her yard. I told him he was just the person I was looking for and started in on him.

I pointed out that he hadn't told me the landing had been driven through the night before Destry was accused of it. I told him the tracks didn't even match Destry's tires. His Explorer, a full-time, all-wheel drive vehicle, had all terrain tires and the tracks in the yard were clearly made by a passenger car tire. He disagreed. I might as well have been talking to a wall. It was hopeless to argue so I stopped. Next, I pointed out that Destry had an alibi for the time period the damage was supposed to have happened. He responded they didn't really know when it happened since nobody had seen it, so Destry's alibi didn't matter.

Not twenty-four hours before, when he delivered Destry home, Staley stated unequivocally there was an eyewitness to the event, the vehicle was known to be a green Explorer, and that the tire tracks matched Destry's vehicle. Now he was saying not only was there no witness, they didn't even know when the crime happened.

In fact, the owner of the house was unaware of the damage until SPD stopped and pointed it out to them. Right after that, the cops saw Destry's vehicle, so it was obvious he was the culprit, still hanging around the scene of the crime hours after the fact. They hadn't even interviewed the kids that were in the vehicle with Destry. Eventually, they would attempt to blame him for everything that had happened in the general neighborhood from the entire previous week.

If I was mad before, I was livid now. I had sense to walk away but, as a parting comment, told Officer Staley they were "fucking idiots". He volunteered as I was stalking off that a small, white car had been seen causing the damage the first night. I didn't even acknowledge the moron. For what it's worth, Staley has since been fired from SPD for allegedly illegal behavior involving domestic violence.

The next day, a Monday, I went down to the police station and discovered that Staley's inability to make elemental observations was a pervasive trait in the department. Two different officers were unwilling to render an answer to a simple yes/no question. I had two photos. One of Destry's tire tracks and one of the yard. Do these tracks look the same to you? You'd have thought I asked them the speed of light.

I pointed out to one, Deputy Police Chief Carson Mansfield, a fellow church member, that the four other kids in the car hadn't even been interviewed. Mansfield knew Destry well and, having taken an oath at Destry's baptism to look after him as his own, I had hopes we'd get to the heart of the matter. Later that evening, one of the occupants of Destry's vehicle was picked up at his house and given a personal tour of the jail and pressured to give Destry up. That's how they interview minors in Salina. It got them nowhere.

If left to Mansfield, I would like to think we would have gotten it resolved, but wishful thoughts are useless when dealing with SPD. Unfortunately, he works for a pompous, narcissist named Jim Hill. Two days later, on Wednesday, we were notified the case was proceeding to trial. Part of me was incredulous but not very much. I was beginning to get the idea of how things worked down at the cop shop.

That evening, I was surprised to get a phone call from Ryan, an acquaintance of Destry from school. I knew a lot of kids, but I knew Ryan better than some because I was a Cubmaster and Ryan spent five years graduating from the rank of Tiger Cub to Webelo in Cub Scouts. He went on to Boy Scouts, excelled, and attained Eagle Scout status, the highest rank possible and earned by very few. He was calling with a story that boggled his virtuous mind.

Ryan had heard Destry was accused of criminal destruction of property for the yard incident. He knew Destry hadn't done it because he heard another kid at school bragging about it. Ryan went to visit the School Resource Officer (SRO) but he wasn't there, so he left a note detailing what he knew. Ryan went back again later but again, the SRO was nowhere to be found. Ryan noticed his note crumpled up in the trash can.

They weren't dealing with an ordinary kid. It's not that easy to get rid of an Eagle Scout. Figuring the guy at the school was just a low level peon, Ryan called SPD that night, just before talking to me, and located the supervisor familiar with the case. He told the supervisor what he knew. The response floored him. "Give it up kid. We've got the one we want."

He hung up and called me immediately. He simply couldn't believe the police would do something like that. I agreed we were all learning a lot, and then asked him who the actual culprit was. He told me it was Brian. He was sure. I thanked him for doing the right thing. I asked Destry if he knew Brian and he replied sure, in fact he'd seen him out driving around that night. Destry's bunch had even followed Brian's car around for awhile. He remembered this because one of the guys in the back seat of Brian's car was the school quarterback, a big, tall kid that looked back at them more than once during the pursuit.

I picked up the phone book. I called the quarterback's parents, who I knew pretty well. Their son was a really good kid and I hated to bring up the whole topic, but I did and asked if they would exert some parental pressure and see what the story was. I then found Brian's address and took a little drive by the house. In the open garage was a small, white car. I pulled in briefly and noted the license tag number.

The QB's mom called back and stated that their son had indeed been with Brian on that Friday night. He admitted that at one point, Brian, probably trying to show off for his audience, drove through a yard. I don't think he impressed anybody. Though students were out of school on both Thursday and Friday of that week, he was positive it was a Friday night. Had it been Thursday night, the night before a big game, there was no way his parents would have let him stay out all night. He, and others, were with Brian in his car on Friday night after the game.

Recalling what Officer Staley told me, this was all very instructive. Staley had stated a small, white car had been seen causing the damage the first night, a Thursday. Yet the QB was saying when he accompanied Brian, it was definitely a Friday night. It was little wonder both sets of tire tracks appeared to have been made by the same vehicle. It had been the same vehicle.

Before school the next morning, I went and parked down the street from Brian's and gave him a call. I stated I was investigating damage caused to a yard in the neighborhood and understood he had information about it. He responded he didn't know anything about it. I immediately replied, "Isn't your license tag" such and such. Taken aback, he slowly responded that yes, it was. I said I thought so. I then asked him if he was aware an innocent person was being blamed for the crime.

This truly seemed to come as news to him. He asked who. I told him Destry Allen. As if it made any difference, he stated he didn't even know who that was. I pointed out that was hardly relevant. What was relevant was that he take responsibility for his actions. I knew his parents were divorced and he lived with his mom. I appealed to him to take control of the situation so his mom wouldn't have to go to the jail and bail him out. Surely, he didn't want to disappoint her. He agreed to go talk to the SRO.

As we ended the call, the garage door on his house, which had been open, closed. It looked like he had decided not to go to school for awhile. That was fine with me. I would let him catch his breath and come back to check with him that afternoon. I did stop by later to talk to him. He stated that he had talked to the SRO and confessed, with the QB in attendance as well. The SRO just took his statement and didn't ask any questions.

One would think that would be the end of Destry's travails. Not only was Destry falsely accused, I, personally, had to catch the culprit because SPD refused to. I haven't been involved in a lot of law enforcement cases so I don't really know how things are normally done, but as a regular citizen, I was left totally repulsed and disgusted. I wrote to Chief Hill and politely pointed out the laws his men broke, that I had to catch the criminal myself, and it really wasn't even that complicated. I stated that I appreciated it was a tough job, but the police really shouldn't be breaking the laws the rest of us are expected to obey. I ended expressing a hope it wouldn't happen again.

The letter just pissed off Hill. How dare anyone criticize his men? Surely, everyone knew that we just lived in his town. It wasn't ours. It was common knowledge Hill had been after the teenagers of Salina ever since his dream that his son play quarterback on the high school team was shot down years before. His son, a bully, much like his father, was told he wasn't going to get the quarterback position on the football team just because he thought he was special. Chief Hill doesn't like to be told no.

There was another interesting side effect of my letter to Hill. Apparently, whenever a complaint is made against the police department, Internal Affairs is required to investigate. One day, I got a phone call from Officer Geary from IA, asking questions regarding the case. Conscious of the fact the call was being recorded, I asked Geary if he was aware another boy had confessed to the crime. He knew nothing about it. I thanked him for going on record with the information.

Geary had one last question. He casually asked if it was true I called Officer Staley a fucking idiot? Just as casually, I responded no, I had not called Staley a fucking idiot. I would never single a man out like that. I stated I had said they were all fucking idiots. Geary politely thanked me for my time. I found it to be a satisfying moment.

Eventually, Hill wrote back and stated his men were exemplary, how dare I call his men fucking idiots, and it was obvious Destry was guilty. However, if Destry were to come pass a polygraph test, he would recommend the case be dropped and apologize personally. Though Destry was actually acquitted, Hill never apologized. As I said, a pompous narcissist. And apparently one that felt his butt was covered a little better than it actually was.

You've got to respect a guy for backing his men at least, even if they constantly screw up. During Hill's tenure, his men have accidentally shot a suspect, accidentally shot themselves, and had at least one man die without explanation while in their custody. That's just the tip of the iceberg. Without doubt, Hill is in charge of a scary bunch.

Not much is seen publicly of Hill these days. Ever since he had a press conference to announce they had apprehended the killer in a relatively high profile homicide case, except it wasn't the killer. In fact, the cops had never even interviewed several of the residents of the neighborhood, who could have told them who did it. When Hill's men finally figured out they had screwed up, the actual suspect was apprehended in short order.

Even then, it took the prosecutor, Ellen Mitchell, three trials to convict the kid. Hill doesn't do any breaking news press conferences anymore after he came across as a publicity hungry racist.

In short, Destry's case wasn't over. Brian was sentenced for causing the damage on Thursday night, but not for Friday, even though a deaf, dumb, and blind man could see he was responsible for both. They conveniently forgot about the QB's statement and Brian, understandably, didn't really have the desire to clarify. Having been found guilty of the crime on Thursday night, he paid to repair all the damage caused during both nights. Officially, it left Friday open to pursue Destry, even though there wasn't any damage left to repair.

Through several continuances, the charges kept getting reduced and we kept rejecting them. One day at a hearing, our attorney, Julie, visibly distressed, pulled me to the side and stated the case was a lot more complicated than we knew. Just before I had arrived, she had asked the prosecutor why they were pursuing the case at all. He replied they had to because Chief Hill had forbid them from dropping the case, no matter what. Having served as county prosecutor in the past, this information came as quite a shock. As a matter of law, the police aren't allowed to run the prosecutor's office, de facto or otherwise. We proceeded into the courtroom.

One of the requests we had on the table was to see the official reports generated by the incident. As the file could conceivably contain other information not related to our case, Judge Robertson needed to review the file and determine what we could see. As the court came into session, he asked our attorney if she had gotten the file. She replied she had.

The judge's next question was telling. Did we get all of it? Julie replied she believed we had, but wouldn't really be able to tell. The judge asked her to let him look at it to make sure the prosecutor had sent it all, as it wouldn't have surprised him if they had kept part of it. Especially the altered police reports by one of the cops, Officer McFadden, evidence of official misconduct, and the details indicating Destry was innocent. He was not a happy man and the prosecutor didn't help the situation by confessing he had only been given the case the day before and had a funeral the same day, so he wasn't prepared. He needed another continuance.

The judge granted his continuance, but warned him that if the prosecution didn't get their act together, he would dismiss the case with prejudice. The next court date found the prosecution poorly prepared, likely by design. At an evidentiary hearing, a synopsis of the case they would present made their case sound idiotic. They had witnesses, but the witnesses hadn't seen anything. They had an expert, but his testimony would amount to agreeing that tires are black. After listening to their case, or more accurately lack of one, the real question was why were we there in the first place?

Julie stood and motioned for acquittal basis the prosecution didn't even have a shred of a case. The judge agreed and it was over. An attorney for over twenty years, our counsel sat in shock. She'd made that motion many, many times over the years and had never had one granted. She asked the judge if that was it. Judge Robertson volunteered he supposed he could walk her client to the car if she wanted, but short of that, he was done.

As far as the prosecution was concerned, it was a success. They had cost us a couple thousand dollars and at the last minute, torpedoed their own case so all of the illegal activity on their part got swept under the rug. They had taught us who was boss. They had made one huge mistake though. Smug as they left the courtroom that day, the prosecutor didn't know that one of her underlings had admitted they couldn't drop the case without the OK of the Chief Hill. You don't have to have spent a career in legal work to know that prosecuting people for a crime with full knowledge they didn't commit it isn't only illegal, it's a violation of constitutional rights.

I asked our attorney if the type of behavior we witnessed in Destry's case was typical. She replied it was more often than not. To me, it sure seemed egregious and I was left wondering what the other residents of Salina, especially the poor, could possibly do to fight such a machine if it went after them.

I'd lived in Salina nearly all of my life and presumed to take at least a modicum of ownership in the town. It seemed to me that I shouldn't, nor anybody else, have to put up with such brazen harassment and corruption from our officials. Basis this, we intended on filing a million dollar lawsuit against the county and the offending officials for slander and malicious prosecution. The white collar law firm we used were so excited to be part of cleaning up our little abscess on the plains they took the case at half their normal rate. They viewed it as an easy kill. I think, as true representatives of the legal professional, they were even more nauseated by the situation than I was. They'd heard of small town justice but never actually seen it at work before.

Our goal wasn't the money. I wanted Hill gone. He was, and is, a blight on our community. Through business, I had learned that there are many forces at work when a decision is made, sometimes not so obvious to the public. One of the forces is insurance companies. They're the ones that pay legal settlements, which they don't really like to do. They would prefer that circumstances be modified to minimize the chance of being in lawsuits, or if it's too late, any more lawsuits. They encourage the type of behavior they like to see via the rate they charge. In simple terms, if an entity is deemed to be a bad risk, the rates go up. It's just like your automobile insurance. The same process is at work in your local government encouraging proper, legal behavior.

As far as I was concerned, the city could keep their corrupt employees, but it was likely going to cost them an arm and a leg to do so if our suit was successful. Chief Hill wasn't popular with some of the city leaders already. Hopefully, we could make the decision to give him his walking papers an easy one, unless they wanted to pay us and our lawyers a boat load of money and, additionally, watch the insurance rates go through the roof in response to keeping a known, proven risk.

Two weeks after alerting the county of our intentions, Destry was killed and his death was swept under the rug by the county and the prosecutor, the same prosecutor that likely would have had her career trashed. The lawsuit went away with Destry's death. It was back to business as usual in Salina, Kansas.

Chapter 12

The civil lawyer we had decided to use met with Saline County officials at the end of December and presented the information that had been gathered over the last six months. I didn't go for fear it would exacerbate the situation. They had little to say other than they felt they had done their jobs, except for the part where they broke the law by not having an autopsy performed and the part where they didn't interview the kid that was involved. They remembered Ray well from the river incident.

Ellen Mitchell, the county prosecutor, volunteered that they knew there was something wrong with Ray when they interviewed him after the river tragedy. He had acted the same as he had at Adam's funeral, completely despondent and overwrought with grief. His performance was so over the top that as the prosecutor and a deputy watched him staggering to his car, the deputy remarked to her Ray would kill himself by the end of the day if his act was genuine.

The last thing they said to our attorney was they would have to be careful in timing their interrogation of Ray because he would likely just lawyer up. For the record, he wouldn't have. He loved to talk and always figured he could massage his way out of most anything. It had worked for him all of his life. More to the point, he would have thought it looked suspicious to ask for an attorney. People like him always do. Why would he need a lawyer if he hadn't done anything wrong?

Mitchell isn't a respected prosecutor. It would surprise most if she could consistently convict the sun of rising in the morning. How competent can anyone be that's so gutless to allow the police chief to call the shots in her office? Combined with the lawsuit that had been looming before Destry's death, I had to wonder just how much her heart was in it. The fact was, the killer had done her a huge, huge favor. Additionally, one didn't have to work for the FBI to figure out they had little hope of convicting anyone with the information available at the time, even if a competent prosecutor did occupy the office. Acknowledging our claims could potentially head down the slippery slope of negligence, a non-insurable risk.

And that was the end of that. We never heard another word from them, ever. Did they ever interview Ray? Your guess is as good as mine. Once they figured out the body had been cremated and most of the evidence was gone, regardless of the fact that they were the ones that destroyed it, they slammed the door. In the shows on television, the victim's family is always treated with dignity, kept in the information loop. Not in Saline County. The rule here is victim's families are lepers.

Chapter 13

During the first two months of 2005, we waited around for the authorities to do whatever it was they were going to do, if anything. They collected oral swabs from Theresa and me. After all, they didn't even know if it was Destry's blood on the gun. I didn't know what they were going to do with the information, but obviously, determining whether the blood on the gun was Destry's might be a step in the right direction. If they did anything other than collect our DNA, we were unaware of it. It distinctly felt like they were just going through the paces.

There were a couple other things we were forced to do that I can only describe as making the short list for parents' worst nightmares. When KBI got involved briefly, they requested any DNA samples from Destry we might have. The list includes anything with saliva, hair with a root, and blood. Theresa and I delivered items personally to KBI. They included a dental retainer, a stocking hat, and baby teeth. Sometimes as a parent you find yourself collecting things you don't know what to do with, but you don't want to get rid of, like baby teeth. It was sobering to realize that, ultimately, we saved Destry's teeth for his homicide investigation.

KBI at least acted like professionals. Agent Mike Van Stratton was respectful and honest, but he played it close to the vest. He, and others in the building, had never seen such incompetent law enforcement. Not a single person had ever heard of a case where law enforcement refused to do an autopsy on a minor. Van Stratton confided that usually one didn't find that poor of a caliber of work, even in Wichita County, out in western Kansas. The entire county has less than five percent of the population of Saline County. It left me wondering what in the world had happened out there.

Van Stratton gave us information that we already knew before we got there. The Saline County SO had screwed up the case so terribly, there was little hope of salvaging it. He made a comment that a right handed person, such as Destry, wouldn't have left the gun in the orientation it was found. Van Stratton committed to doing whatever they could do to help bring closure to our family. We weren't looking for closure. We were more interested in justice. In addition to the personal items we left, the chair I had found last fall with the blood spatter was turned over to them for examination. Since I didn't believe the SO trustworthy, I had been withholding it in my home.

The second thing we did can only be described as horrifyingly educational. It's something no parent should ever be forced to do. We purchased an educational video set used by law enforcement. The subject matter? Analyzing gunshot wounds to determine, among other things, the distance weapons were fired from victims. I know it sounds horrendously gruesome, and it was, but it was presented in a professional manner. The subject matter was truly interesting, if not macabre.

One of the problems we faced with the abundance of information we had was to decide who actually knew what they were talking about. The Saline County Coroner, Dr. Allred, swore Destry was shot point blank, the muzzle of the barrel against the skin. Incidentally, that type of wound can just as easily be achieved by someone else firing the gun. You don't have to shoot yourself to be shot point blank.

Our forensic pathologist, nationally renowned, contended Destry's head wound indicated he was shot from an indeterminate distance, meaning over two feet away, and the bullet had fragmented into pieces due to a defect in the gun. When discussing this aspect of the report with SPD's expert on weapons and ammunition, he referred to revolvers with this tendency to mangle bullets as lead spitters. It was a common type of defect in poorly made weapons, one that even SPD's expert knew about. He commented it was especially common in cheap pistols made in Germany during a certain era. Our pistol was cheap, German, and from that era.

A person can be shot from three different classifications of distance. Point blank, intermediate, and indeterminate. The indications of each type of wound have distinctly unique characteristics. It's not that we doubted our expert, the guy who actually knew what he was doing with the curriculum vitae to back him up. It wasn't his part time job. Allred had gone to one class, total, and only had the job because the county couldn't find anyone else to fill the position. As a general practitioner, his expertise was in runny noses, not forensic science.

We just wanted to know what they were basing their observations on. As I mentioned, my interest was already piqued by my untrained observations of Destry's wound and the employee who had shot himself in the forehead. We watched the video. We learned a lot of details that do happen to come in handy when watching cop shows. We also found out that, no surprise, our expert seemed to know what he was talking about.

One other realization began to emerge. The nauseating reality that authorities were under no obligation to investigate anything and if they didn't do their job, there was little recourse to getting to the truth. As elected officials, both the county prosecutor and the sheriff answer to nobody but the voters.

Without the long arm of the law, why would anyone submit to interviews when we asked? Discussions with retired law enforcement professionals confirmed this belief. Unless we could get Ray into court for some reason, we would be unable to proceed. There were two ways to get into court. One was the way we were trying, going after him and hoping someone would take notice.

There was another way of course. Get him to take us to court. In other words, provoke a lawsuit.

I'm not a criminal and I try to limit my interactions with the law to the occasional speeding ticket. Suggesting I break the law on purpose went against my grain, even if it was necessary for the big picture. I'd never been in trouble for anything, so no matter what I did, it wasn't likely I would get in too much trouble as a first time offender. Of course, Ray would have to be incredibly stupid to take the bait and go into court on purpose. As luck would have it, I didn't even have to do anything. It seemed Ray was incredibly stupid and saved me the trouble of even provoking him.

Chapter 14

Jessie

We met Jessie McWhirt in late March of 2004, during the time period between Adam's death and Destry's death. At the time, she was a senior in high school. She began coming to the house with Ray on his visits. She was an odd girl, but given who she was with, it didn't surprise any of us. Ray would just walk in unannounced whenever he happened to come by, always to get some cash, and she would follow him in. Jessie literally hid behind him every time they came. Everyone commented on it. I've never observed behavior quite like it in my life. The strange thing was that after Destry died, she never came with him to our house again.

They were quite a little couple, him shirtless in his silk smoking jacket adorned with a big cross necklace and her awkwardly hiding behind him. When we forced her to speak, she found her voice and explained she was going into the United States Air Force in the fall and that her father was a general at Fort Riley, about forty-five miles east of Salina. She wasn't terribly unpleasant to look at and save a pronounced overbite and obvious self image problem, didn't appear too bad of a catch. We had always wondered what type of woman Ray would end up with, given his tendency to lie, cheat, steal, etc. The ones he had always wanted were so far beyond his reach, it was truly sad, so we were warily happy for Ray. As we would eventually find out, Ray and Jessie were meant for each other. One of our lawyers put it best when he said that in his experience, people like them always seem to find each other.

The best way for the reader to envision Jessie is to refer to the popular television show *Cops*. The scenario: Law enforcement responds to a domestic disturbance call at a trailer park. When they arrive, they find a man and a woman in the front yard beating the crap out of each other. The cops struggle to separate them, focusing on the man who they probably assume is the aggressor. However, as they restrain him they find themselves pummeled from behind by a bleeding woman screaming, "Leave my man alone!! I love him!!" Mix that together with the emotional maturity of a five-year-old and you've got Jessie.

Jessie was especially proud of her ability to keep up with her brothers when it came time to smack each other. She fancied herself quite a puncher and had the personality of a badger to boot. Most aren't aware, but when a badger is crossing a road and a car comes along threatening to run him over, he will actually stop to take on the vehicle. The results are predictable, but badgers don't care. As with Jessie, it's in their nature. My sister, Brenda, Ray's mother, even commented to me she was worried about how Ray and Jessie hit each other. They would have contests to see who could hit the other in the arm the hardest. The winner was the one that didn't say stop. Jessie always won.

As it turned out, not too surprisingly, she was a capable liar herself and not exactly a brain trust to boot. Her father wasn't a general or anything even close. He was in the National Guard in Salina. When she lied, she was so vociferous, even I was tempted to believe her, knowing full well she was lying. In Jessie's case, I ultimately found myself concluding she believed most of her own lies through her blind gullibility. Plus, she really wanted to believe what she proclaimed.

One of my favorites was when Ray and Jessie got married in March of 2006. In an interview, she told investigators none of her family would come to the wedding because they had heard that Theresa and I were going to ambush the ceremony with assault weapons and kill them all. Most would hesitate to even say anything so ludicrous to an actual person, much less to investigators in a homicide case. In actuality, none of her family approved of Ray in any way, shape, or form which, in Jessie's adversarial mindset, was the best reason of all to marry him.

Another one of my favorites had to do with why she would come with Ray to our house. Even though it was the most ludicrous lie imaginable, it didn't mean she didn't believe it. Though both she and Ray never missed an opportunity to create lies that would serve to smear my name, this one set a new bar for comedy relief. When asked by the same investigators why she never went to our house after Destry's death, she responded she only went with Ray to our house in the first place because it would aid Ray in getting money. I would get so caught up and distracted admiring her fine breasts that I would give Ray anything he wanted. When one of the investigators, Kathern, asked if this was an effective ploy, Jessie chuckled and responded very proudly that, indeed, it worked every time.

According to her, he never got any before she went. That wasn't true, but Jessie was never much of one for the details. She truly believed what she was saying. Not surprisingly, it was Ray's idea. Not only did it stroke her fragile ego, it made her feel like he needed her.

Though in the recordings made at the time it sounds like the investigators were laughing with her, they weren't. When they arrived back at our house after the interview, they had planned on accusing me of being a dirty old man with straight faces, but they couldn't carry it off. I would be the first to admit I certainly have nothing against nice breasts, but in my opinion, which is the only one that matters in her scenario, Jessie wouldn't be defined as being a member of that club. Quite honestly, my only memory of her during those visits was her defining characteristic of cowering behind Ray all the time. I was apparently totally oblivious to the provocative dress she referred to.

Jessie hated family and often criticized Ray for having had any faith in family in the first place. One of Ray's pillars of principle was that we should just believe what he had to offer and not question his answers because that's what family does. He, therefore, didn't feel he had any obligation to speak further with us due to this most basic injustice. Jessie would tell him it was his own fault for ever believing in family in the first place. Of course, in actuality, he never did. To Ray, family members had always been just convenient dupes.

She also never missed an opportunity to be rude and insulting. In fact, she would more often than not go out of her way to do so. As she described herself to Gary, a polygraph examiner, ".. they got a good dose of me, I'm not a sweet cookie cake thing. I was mean." Though she clearly bastardized some saying, one gets the idea. I was a creepy old man with a wandering eye for young girls like her and Theresa was a cold, gutter mouth, always wired and from a long line of druggies and drunks. We were both emotionless. Bear in mind, we saw her on maybe four occasions for a total of a half hour. As with every other thing that came out of her mouth, she was quite informed and proud to tell anyone that would stand still long enough to listen.

The following story illustrates my point about her gullibility when it came to Ray and his wild manifestations. In the month before Destry's death, Ray had become enamored and sexually involved with a fifteen-year-old he briefly worked with. Jessie didn't consider it to be cheating on her because she and Ray weren't together as a couple at the time, though she didn't know it. What?

Ray had broken up with her at the beginning of May in such a way she failed to get the message, so she wasn't aware they had broken up. Ray seemed to be pretty clear on the issue and immediately got together with someone else, or more likely already was with them. The fact the girl was a minor was a mere technicality. Jessie and Ray continued to have sexual relations at the same time, or as Jessie put it in retrospect, they were apparently just friends with favors. In discussing the topic in the interview, she blamed herself completely for not understanding Ray when he broke up with her. It wasn't Ray's fault. To listen to her, she was just a dumb, unworldly girl, but one that knew about pretty much everything else otherwise. It was pretty clear Ray was filling in whatever blanks there were.

All in all, she was just mean, spiteful, and opinionated. The phrase "I don't know" wasn't in her vocabulary. Even Ray saw it as her defining attribute. At a stalking hearing, one initiated by Ray and Jessie, she put so much effort into being a bulldog, it was all our lawyer could do to restrain himself in a professional manner. At one point, when he put it to her directly that she didn't have any proof whatsoever I was to blame for whatever things were happening to them, she responded she just knew. After all, she declared, nobody else in Salina didn't like them. He couldn't resist any longer and replied, "You want to bet?" When we eventually responded to their lawsuit with our own malicious prosecution case, she stated she could sort of understand it because she had looked up malicious and she agreed. She had been mean in court and proud of it. Like I said, not exactly a brain trust.

At another point, she replied to a question regarding the number of times she had observed me following her as being countless. Getting fed up with her attitude, our lawyer declared he thought she could count pretty high. Did she agree? Of course she could, Jessie replied. Ultimately, after a much needed lesson in mathematics from our attorney, countless turned into two times and those occurrences, even she agreed, were dubious.

I always felt sorry for Jessie to a degree. I don't know what her life had been like growing up, but clearly she was so desperate for love, she was willing to believe anything Ray would say, even with full knowledge that he lied constantly to everyone. She even caught him in lies over and over and still wanted to believe.

Jessie saw herself as Ray's protector from the terrible world she had always known about, one Ray had only recently come to know. Toward the end of the investigation, under questioning by another seasoned investigator, she even bragged of her peripheral but pivotal involvement in Ray's life and defense, bragging she was "the door". Without her, nobody could get to him.

Our pursuit of the truth and Ray never had anything to do with Jessie and I personally think most in her position would take every opportunity to stay clear, but that was never the case with her. At the end, she genuinely seemed offended we had never had any interest in her, only Ray. From day one, she wanted it to be her fight and saw it as her fight, mostly because she just liked to fight.

Bart & Theresa Allen in front of the Depot. (Courtesy of Salina Journal Newspaper)

Bart Allen debating Saline County Sheriff Glen Kochanowski in county elections during the fall of 2008. (Courtesy of Salina Journal Newspaper)

Theresa Allen pleading with the Saline County Commission to not renew the contract of Saline County Coroner, Dr. Charles Allred. (Courtesy of Salina Journal Newspaper)

The broken screen door on the Depot as found the morning of Destry's death.

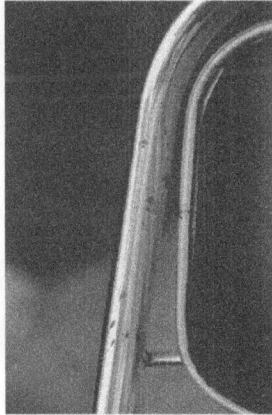

Chair with blood spatter found by Bart Allen (front view of backrest).

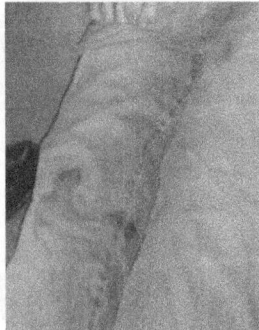

Unexplained blood stain on the front of Destry's jeans, right knee area.

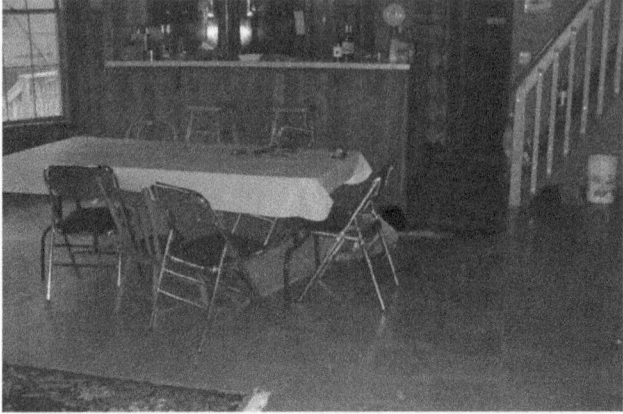
The crime scene (note: stairs to loft on right).

The Allen family (from left- Ransom, Destry, Theresa, Bart, Lucas).

Destry Allen (right) & Ray Jones, April, 2004.

A Pristine Suicide

Destry Greer Allen.

Destry & Nichole.

Bart Allen on the first anniversary of Destry's death.

Chapter 15

There was a saying when I was a kid back in the 1960' s. Paranoia will destroy ya'. I didn't know if Ray had ever heard of the saying, but I knew he was the living proof that such modicums were rooted in some sort of eternal truth. In the middle of March, 2005, he filed a protection from stalking order against me.

Now, had he been a normal person under normal circumstances and had I actually been doing something to provoke his belief I was stalking him, it might have been a prudent move. But I wasn't stalking him. In fact, I was going out of my way to stay away from him since I had a belief that somewhere in the background, the SO was actually conducting an investigation. Not only was I nowhere near him, presumably he was the subject of a murder investigation. In response, he decided to attack me.

It seemed a bold and, as it appeared later, bizarrely calculated move. Somewhere before the first of March, Ray and Jessie had moved to a new address, a rental house, from the apartment they had occupied since early summer the year before. They wanted to have a house with a yard so they could get a dog, which they did, and named it Trigger. It was an odd name for a golden retriever, especially given what Ray was being accused of. Like the physical move to a new house, it seemed as though he was throwing sand in our faces.

With nearly fifty thousand residents, there are a lot of places to live in Salina. Out of the entire city, they chose to move into a house that happened to be on the most direct route to two significant destinations for our family on a daily basis - our youngest son's school and my place of employment. This wasn't a simple feat to accomplish since we only lived a mile from the school and there are only around five rental houses between the school and our house.

Without knowing it, we had been driving by their new rental a couple of times a day during the school and work week for quite awhile before I noticed his truck parked in the driveway one day in February. Where I worked and where Lucas went to school were certainly not secrets to Ray, since his dad had worked at the same place. If a person was to believe what he said, they had simply moved and I had all of a sudden, out of the blue, started stalking them, mysteriously in the morning, around noon, and late afternoon.

One notable and very relevant event occurred just before they filed for protection from stalking. The local newspaper, the *Salina Journal*, decided to run a story about Ray on the anniversary of the river rafting tragedy. The title? *Reclaiming a Life*. It featured Ray, on the front page, gazing pensively out over the river at the spot the tragedy took place. Little did the reporter, Sharon, realize she was providing a platform for the Ray show. He was interviewed and allowed to spin his tales, and spin he did. If Sharon had taken the time to look at the coverage in their own paper from a year before, she would have noticed his creative embellishments. I sent the editor an email and informed him of their problem.

When I went to talk in person with the editor, he volunteered immediately they hadn't vetted the story properly and they had already been in touch with their lawyers. I wasn't so concerned with the contradictions in the news story as I was

Ray's sudden clarity on the manner in which Adam had died. The details he provided would have certainly caused distress for Adam's family and I thought the paper should know the result of their actions.

Few people can speak authoritatively about a child's death, other than those that have been through the experience themselves. When your child dies, you hope death was quick with no suffering. I know it was important to me. The initial reports seemed to indicate Adam went down fast, bolstered by Ray's comment from the year before that he never saw him. As a parent, you couldn't hope for much better, given the circumstances.

But after a year of romanticizing the event, Ray's memory was eloquent and moving. It was also quite likely a nightmare if you were Adam's parents. Not only did their son drown, he had a lot of time to think about it. All the while, according to Ray's warped revelations, Adam's thoughts weren't with survival or those he was leaving behind. They were with Ray.

Right after the accident, Ray told the authorities he never saw Adam. They went over some small falls located upstream from the bigger ones, capsized, and Adam went under. That was it. A year later, his memory had suddenly become much clearer. Not only had he seen Adam after they capsized, according to Ray, Adam clung to the raft, snagged on a log, for two minutes. Ray managed to get on top of a logjam and looked over at Adam, struggling in the rampaging water. According to the Journal, Ray recalled the following.

> "The look I'll never forget is the look on his face,"
> Ray said. "He cared more about what was going to
> happen to me than what was happening to himself.
> I said, 'I'm all right. I'm all right.'"

It's hard to believe Adam's greatest concern, hanging on for dear life, freezing in thirty-eight degree water, was whether Ray was going to be okay. It wouldn't have been mine. Ray went on.

> "After about two minutes, he just disappeared,"

Ray said. "That's when it really hit me. I knew I had
to do what I could, myself, to survive. I knew that I
had to survive, to tell the story. To tell his parents.
His family had to know."

Not only was his memory drastically different, it was now a
compelling, heartwarming story in the midst of chaos and
despair. The whole story of their relationship, culminating in
Adam's death was downright gooey. They were basically boy
scouts, living for the natural goodness life had to offer.

Ray stated he had been running nine miles a day using a
Navy Seals workout daily. He had sworn off drugs from his high
school days. They sailed boats made from post-it notes while
approaching their demise at the falls. According to Ray, they
planned to paddle all the way back to the beginning, to get a
good workout, but their fascination with the post-it note boats
caused them to miss the huge bridge that signaled it was time to
turn back upstream. Given the state of the river that day, it
wouldn't have been possible to even beach the raft, much less
paddle back to their starting point.

It was quite a life affirming story, the kind they like to put
on Sunday morning newspapers, and a complete, absurd lie. For
instance, Ray neglected to mention the marijuana the authorities
found in his backpack out on the logjam, though he was quick to
point out to the reporter about how he never did drugs. That
little detail would've ruined the whole feel of the story I'm sure.

After Adam died, Ray went on to explain his state of mind
in the following weeks.

"I was nothing," he said. "It was complete emptiness.
I wasn't sad. I wasn't happy. I wasn't regretful. I wasn't
mournful. I wasn't anything."

Though only a snapshot out of Ray's life, it summed up
everything we had already figured out on our own after a
lifetime of watching him. Ray was a narcissistic sociopath,
lacking any semblance of a conscience. All of his life was a
storybook that revolved completely around him. Everything

happened to him, not others. As he had proclaimed after Destry's death, "Why does this keep happening to me?" He went on to explain to Sharon that it was only his cousin's suicide three months later that brought him out of the mist, that woke him from his sleepwalk.

In his quest to glorify his exploits, I'm sure it never once occurred to him, and wouldn't have mattered if it had, that he was exponentially amplifying the grief of suffering parents on the first year anniversary of their son's death. Why would he care? It was all about him. The article only served to embolden Ray and his righteous behavior. After all, he had beaten the system and his stupidity was now being glorified, once again, for the whole city to see.

The SO served me with a summons for a court appearance related to the stalking suit several days after the news article. I found it all strangely amusing. I was being accused of stalking the person I believed shot my son in cold blood and the specter of the cops serving me for doing something wrong in the big picture was an absurd, perverse joke.

Of note, when I asked the officers that were serving me whether a guy should take a lawyer to court for this type of thing, they laughingly responded that most didn't. They were just some good ole' boys, they were, and if I were anyone else, I suppose, their lackadaisical attitude wouldn't have mattered. As it was, I didn't find ignorant cops that fantasized they were clever to be that amusing.

At the time, I was pretty sure they were recording the conversation. Otherwise, why send two dunces to do the job of one? Indeed, they were. Cops always do. The recording was sent to Ellen Mitchell, the county prosecutor, at her request. Why did she have any interest in Ray's stalking suit? The SO and Mitchell were eager to help Ray or, more likely, were out to get me. How would recording me conceivably be to my benefit in the stalking matter? It wouldn't. Not only that, the case number listed on the transcript of the conversation indicated it was part of Destry's file, not the stalking suit. Out to get the dad of the dead kid. What a great use of county resources. It was just plain pathetic.

In the transcript, they seem disappointed I didn't help them. Of course, when it got to the court date, when potential information about a possible homicide might be developed, they were nowhere to be found. They couldn't care less about justice. Their motives were clear. Make it go away, take me down, or hopefully, both.

When the stalking matter got to court, Ray didn't appear to understand what he had gotten himself into or, for that matter, that he could make it go away just as easily by standing up and declaring he was dropping the complaint. It was filed by him, of his own accord. There was no law enforcement involved compelling him to go forward with the suit or to testify. I think it's safe to say if he had brought a lawyer, many things would have turned out differently.

From our standpoint, it was a very good thing he didn't. Our lawyer, Stephen Joseph, a seasoned prosecutor, went after both Ray and Jessie like a chicken on a June bug. Judge Hellmer, who had been under the impression this would be another typical protection hearing, appeared taken aback initially. Joseph begged for some latitude from the judge and since Ray and Jessie hadn't brought counsel to object, the judge let him go ahead, though he did caution Joseph about his line of questioning on two occasions. They had absolutely no proof of their bizarre assertions and I was acquitted without even presenting a defense. The outcome had never really been in question and my defense wasn't the reason they were grilled on the stand for over two hours.

Joseph's attack of Ray and Jessie was in their face, brutal, and completely unanticipated. They were there to get me for stalking them. It had never occurred to them they would have to defend themselves. Jessie, never the sharpest tool in the shed, came across as a low class pit bull and was more than happy to rise to the bait. When it came Ray's turn to testify, after having witnessed his girlfriend's dissection, he literally didn't even contend that I had done anything wrong. When given the chance to present his argument of how I was stalking him, he pulled a Rodney King. His only comment was he just wished we could all get along and didn't even make an assertion I had done anything wrong at all.

Two significant pieces of information emerged from their testimony. Ray confessed that he found out about Destry's death at around 9:30 a.m. in the morning on June 10. That was nearly an hour before I had even called emergency services. It was also three hours before he was informed by the pastor at our house, a scene observed by several bystanders. He wasn't asked to explain the discrepancy at the time, or at any time for that matter, though he eventually felt compelled to offer a convoluted story he believed explained the inconsistency. It didn't come close.

The other piece of information was that they had someone with them that night and he was their alibi. This revelation was likely inspired by the information I had supplied Ray back at the visit in September, that his girlfriend wouldn't be enough of an alibi. Jessie and Ray revealed that Tommy was celebrating his birthday with them down at Adam's Cross that night. They both stated they were all together from 9 p.m. until around 3 a.m. As Jessie so eloquently stated when asked what in the world they were doing for seven hours, "We was just sittin' and chillin'." We went looking for Tommy.

Salina's not that big. I asked one of the only kids I knew that had attended the same high school as Jessie, and presumably Tommy. He not only knew Tommy, he knew where he was working and gave me the name of the place. I sent our private detective to visit Tommy at work.

Tommy was downright righteous. He was, indeed, with Ray and Jessie that night for the whole time they said he was. Tommy knew they were going to use his name and it was okay with him. As their friend, he was sick and tired of everybody thinking all this bad stuff about Ray and didn't mind helping them clear their name. The detective, playing on Tommy's desire to help them clear up everything, implored him to speak with Ray and Jessie and get them to agree to an interview, possibly even a polygraph. He agreed.

Initially, Ray, Jessie, and Tommy, in their naivety, believed just naming Tommy as an alibi would end everything. They were with him, simple as that, so that should have been the end of it. Obviously, it wasn't. The detective called Tommy a week later. Tommy's enthusiasm had waned considerably. Ray's reaction to Tommy's suggestion he come forward only angered Ray and drew accusations of stabbing them in their backs. So much for wanting to clear their names. The detective gave him a pep talk and begged him to try again. He agreed.

The detective gave him a few more weeks and called Tommy back. He had quit his full time job, left town, and moved to Manhattan, Kansas, with a sudden impulse to attend college. He hadn't mentioned that was in his plan when he was interviewed a month before. When contacted, he didn't see any need to talk to Ray or clear anyone's name as he wasn't living in Salina anymore and wasn't planning on ever coming back to live.

Tommy's sudden change of heart about clearing everybody's names and hasty departure from the city was suspicious at the very least. We left Tommy alone for the next few months. With little recourse, our detective called Ray directly and appealed to him to take actions to get this behind him.

Our detective suggested Ray and Jessie take a polygraph. Ray had no interest. His position was that he only answered to God and that his family should take his word, no questions asked. He also stated he knew that there was no official investigation going on. He was the one that had been wronged, not us. How dare we not believe him, a person that had never told the truth in his entire life. A person that used people, including family, like toilet paper. A person that hadn't even shed a tear over his cousin's death.

Chapter 16

We were going to let the waters calm after interviewing Ray and Tommy so we could come up with a game plan. The stalking suit was such a joke, it was clear the whole exercise was intended to discredit and silence me and our campaign to catch Destry's killer. Ray hadn't even presented an argument, much less evidence, of my supposed stalking. For her part, Jessie came across as vile, ignorant, and vicious, also lacking any proof of wrongdoing on my part. We filed a malicious prosecution action against both of them.

Some days are better than others for Theresa and me. Hunting down your child's killer, on your own, takes its toll. In addition, the entire process was moving slowly. One day early in June, Theresa couldn't take it anymore and drove to Ray and Jessie's rental house to confront Ray.

Other than my mom, Theresa had been the only constant woman in Ray's life. He went on numerous family vacations with us and practically every holiday was spent, at least briefly, with our family. Ray appears in over three hundred photos in our family photo collection. Whenever Brenda had a breakdown, my mom and Theresa were there. For Ray to simply say he was offended by our accusations and wasn't going to speak with us anymore was akin to a child telling their parents they didn't have any right to ask questions after years of wiping their nose and cleaning their diapers. His arrogance was monstrous.

At first, I was going to let Theresa go and ream him, but it occurred to me that he could well shoot her. I didn't know what type of weapons he had, but we had been informed by a neighbor of Ray's that he was proud of telling those who came to his door that he had a weapon, an AK47, just inside. He indicated to anyone who would listen that he was a hunted man. Ray was the definition of paranoid. Besides, his mental instability made predicting his reaction to anything impossible.

As it turned out, the opposite happened. Theresa did have a verbal confrontation with Jessie. According to her, Ray wasn't home, even though his pickup was in the driveway. Nothing was accomplished. They called SPD to report being threatened and an officer was sent to our house to investigate. It was a non-event except for one revelation from the officer. As I said, they felt threatened.

They? Jessie had said Ray wasn't home. In fact, he was at home. The officer volunteered he had been hiding in the closet during Theresa's visit, afraid of being confronted by his aunt, a 105 pound women. Ray was all man alright.

I hit my own breaking point, of sorts, the same month. Frustrated with the whole process and the emerging reality the SO wasn't going to do anything other than sit on their butts, I felt the need to speak out. The first anniversary of Destry's death, which coincided with the Smoky Hill River Festival, seemed an appropriate time and venue.

With a can of white spray paint, a black t-shirt, some block letters, and a kit of fuchsia hair dye, I created a cost effective marketing package. In anticipation, I had been growing a goatee for the last month. I dyed it fuchsia, spray painted "Salina Pigs Suck" on my black t-shirt, and headed off for the festival, an event attended by tens of thousands of people annually. I was eager to see how the practical application of First Amendment rights was going to work out.

At the time, I was still president of a successful company, a past Cubmaster, and a generally respected, sane member of the community. It was a new look for me, to say the least. I got the impression I scared the crap out of most I knew, mainly because it seemed obvious I had finally gone around the bend. The only people that actually made eye contact or spoke with me were those that wanted to know where they could buy the shirt. I felt I had effectively made my point, for those paying attention.

Around the fourth of July in 2005, Ray did something that couldn't have possibly helped his credibility. Three months after I was acquitted of stalking charges, Ransom and I were moving a 1968 convertible I had been storing out at work. I had intended to refurbish the car many years before, but it never came to pass. It had become more of a storage project than anything else. As we were towing the car, I received a phone call from SPD. An officer inquired if I knew Ray Jones.

Apparently, Ray had called them to complain that I had just tried to run him over as he was walking with Jessie down the street. He told them he had to jump up on the curb to keep me from hitting him. I told the officer I was moving a car and didn't know anything about it and Ray was mentally deranged. That was the end of it.

At that point, Ray must have had quite a file down at SPD. I knew he believed they were his allies and he wasn't afraid to call them for the slightest of irritations. That's the only explanation I could come up with for the lack of investigation. Not that it bothered me, but it occurred to me that if I called and said someone had seriously tried to kill me with their car, I think I would have expected SPD to look into it a little more than to just call and ask the alleged perpetrator if he did it. However, knowing what I now know, their lack of initiative was probably just par for the course.

When I visited the editor of the paper in March related to the story of Ray's redemption, I also took the occasion to fill them in on the bigger story beginning to play out relating to Destry's death. I pointed out to them the hero in their story was the last one to see another young man alive that was found dead three months later and that the SO had, for whatever reason, totally blown the investigation.

I'm sure from time to time they have people like me that come in and make bizarre assertions, but I actually had documents and reports to back me up. Combined with the glaring lies Ray told them in their interview and his coincidental whereabouts in the death of two young men, they eventually felt compelled to look into the whole matter. They didn't take my paperwork, but who could blame them. For all they knew, I had a flair for creative writing.

That summer, Sharon, the same reporter that had documented Ray's fluff story on the river tragedy anniversary, set about trying to authenticate what I was claiming. She called the SO and was denied access to the reports. She sent a letter requesting the documents under the Freedom of Information Act. They sent a letter and said no. That left Sharon with little recourse other than to look at the reports the grieving dad/crazy guy had in his custody.

As they had with us, the reports raised concerns in Sharon's mind, so she called to ask questions. The SO, not particularly happy she had gained access to reports, didn't have any answers to share. The coroner also refused to share anything. She pressed her point with more phone calls until they simply refused to talk to her at all, about anything. It becomes a real problem to report news related to criminal activity if law enforcement refuses to acknowledge your existence. It seemed they pretty much showed the paper who was in control, gambling the story would eventually die and go away, I suspect.

Sharon called Ray to speak with him about his perspective on what was going on. She already knew him after the story she had done on the river tragedy anniversary. Ray didn't want to talk about anything. Most memorable about the phone call was Jessie screaming in the background at Sharon, something to the effect, "We're gonna sue you bitch!" I don't know how much opposition Sharon usually runs into trying to report on a story, but to me, she seemed a little taken aback by the whole thing. The authorities were just about right. The story did almost go away.

Chapter 17

Summer turned into fall. The first of November, 2005, brought a visit from Tommy to our house. We had left him alone since early summer, though he obviously fit into the eventual malicious prosecution lawsuit against Ray and Jessie. Tommy hadn't said which college he was going to attend, but it wasn't really that hard to figure out it was likely Kansas State University since he was living in Manhattan, Kansas, home of KSU. As a lot of college kids do, Tommy created an account on Facebook and listed all that information we were warned not to share back in the 1960's. Consequently, we knew where he was and how to contact him.

Nichole, Destry's girlfriend, also knew how to use Facebook and in the fall, contacted Tommy. A truly sweet person and beautiful young woman, Nichole was able to open a dialogue with him. Tommy had been through a lot of family turmoil in the last year, in addition to being drug into a murder investigation, and was probably a little vulnerable. One weekend afternoon early in November, Nichole called and acknowledged she and Tommy were out driving around and asked if she could bring him over to our house.

I wasn't sure if it was a good idea, from the legal standpoint, since we had a lawsuit pending and he would likely be an important part of it. It occurred to me we were already pretty much off in unchartered waters with the whole situation, so I told her to bring him on over. As expressed over the phone, Tommy's real desire was just to see if we were the animals Ray had described to him. Nichole had been assuring him we were normal parents just looking to get to the bottom of things. He wanted to see for himself.

There were other people at the house when they pulled up. Besides Theresa and myself, there was Ransom and his girlfriend. In other words, there were five persons to witness Tommy's comments. He was a nice enough young man and seemed pretty open about his involvement.

The night of Destry's death, Tommy had indeed spent the evening with Ray and Jessie. It was his birthday and he was bummed out that no one seemed to care and so he ended up with them as sort of a last resort. They had only hung around together since the river incident. As far as Destry was concerned, Tommy had only met him earlier the week he died and he didn't know Destry, other than as somebody that hung with Ray and Jessie. He did admit at first, he thought Ray and Destry were brothers because of the way Ray referred to him in conversation and acted around him. After all, Tommy didn't really know Ray, other than through Jessie.

Tommy had heard about Destry's death while at work the day Destry was found, when Ray and Jessie sought him out to inform him. Since he didn't really even know Destry, the visit caught him off guard, but he did recount that Ray didn't seem too broken up by the news, considering Destry was his cousin. As Tommy had only met him once, it seemed odd they would come to work to tell him. While there, they made arrangements to meet Tommy later for a little partying that evening.

This part of the story illustrates well just how conniving Ray was. When Ray, Jessie, and Tommy got together that night, they made a visit to where I worked, McShares, Inc. As the production plant in the back runs both days and nights, the gate was almost always open. Ray knew this since his father also worked at the same place. Around midnight, while parked in back by the plant, Jerry, a supervisor in the plant, noted the presence of a vehicle. As he was wondering what was going on, Ray got out of his truck and approached Jerry. It's a small business and, as Kim's son, Ray was known to all. Before Jerry could say a word, Ray greeted him and, without hesitation, asked Jerry if he had heard Destry killed himself the night before.

Jerry's knees nearly buckled. He had known Destry since he was born. Not only that, Jerry had two siblings that committed suicide. The news of Destry's death shook him. Ray didn't miss a beat and went on to state that he and his buddies were picking up some firewood that was stored there. Ray stated his uncle, me, knew all about it. Then he left.

Since I was in charge, I'm sure Ray didn't think it was likely anyone would call me in the middle of the night to confirm his story. The bombshell information he gave Jerry made it even more unlikely anyone would call. Jerry, stunned, was still trying to come to grips with the news when Ray walked away. Calling me about such miniscule matters as firewood wasn't on his mind. He recalled that Ray returned about an hour later, presumably to get more firewood.

What really stood out about the episode for Jerry was Ray's lack of emotion when he relayed the disturbing news to him. Jerry knew about death, shocking death at that. Ray didn't seem bothered in the least. His mentioning the death to Jerry wasn't intended as information as much as a diversion from what he really wanted. To steal.

As Ray didn't tell Tommy they were stealing, it never occurred to him that was the purpose of the trip to McShares, so when Tommy told us the story, it also didn't occur to him that he was informing on Ray. We had known about the visit for some time, but didn't know who was with Ray and Jessie. In actuality, they weren't there to get firewood. They were there to steal concrete blocks used for landscaping to make a fire pit out in the country so they could stay warm while they drank.

Of course, the blocks weren't owned by Ray or it wouldn't have been stealing. They were owned by our church. The day I sent Ray to the church to work for his money, I mentioned he did work. His job was to move blocks out of the way for some dirt work. He was told to simply move the blocks aside. True to form, Ray always had a better idea, one that was always to his advantage.

His idea was to put the blocks in his truck, take them to McShares, and store them out of the way. He thought that would show what a great worker he was. I told him, in no uncertain terms, not to. He wasn't volunteering to bring the blocks back, just take them. I would be the one that had to do the additional work. I didn't check or notice until some time later that he had blatantly disregarded what he was instructed to do.

If it were anyone but Ray, it would've been easy to discount the event as a misunderstanding with an over enthusiastic youth. But that's how Ray did things. Life was simply one misunderstanding after another to those who knew Ray. In reality, even as he was working to dig the blocks out at the church, he was already thinking of how he could steal them, since it was obvious they would work well for the fire pits he was making on a regular basis. Even Destry's death wouldn't alter his plans.

Ever since Adam had died, Ray had claimed to be a new person, saved by Jesus Christ himself. He had taken to wearing a weird, silk smoking jacket he bought at goodwill and around his neck, perfectly centered in the V of his jacket, was a cross, often worn without even a t-shirt. He was hugging anyone that would stand still. Ray was Christianity incarnate and he was happy to tell anyone that asked.

Except for one detail. He stole from the church, premeditatedly at that. That's why he lied to Jerry about their intention to get firewood. Several weeks after the initial visit and conversation with Jerry, Ray was again observed at McShares, late at night. When confronted, he stated with conviction that his Uncle Bart had asked him to inventory the blocks. At 1 a.m.? Yeah, right. It was a strange response, but they knew Ray and since no one wanted to call and bother the boss in the middle of the night, the worker left the issue alone and forgot about it.

They didn't get to use the blocks for very long. Tommy stated they were trespassing on land in the country at the time, when car lights approached they abandoned their party scene. During their short time around the fire, Tommy stated Ray didn't seem upset and they didn't even really discuss Destry's demise. So basically, less than twenty-four hours after Destry died, Ray was back to business, lying, stealing, and partying, without any outward appearances of any sort of mourning for his cousin.

Tommy volunteered other details. He stated that Ray felt Destry had everything better than him. Ray felt even Destry's girlfriend was better than his. Tommy also stated that Ray had a hair trigger temper and rage that left most walking on eggs when they were around him. For instance, everyone knew not to ask Ray to repay borrowed money, even a dollar. He also stated that Ray and Jessie's relationship was prone to terrible fights.

As Tommy's visit was ending, we asked him what Ray had told him about Destry's death. Tommy stated Ray said it was a suicide because Destry and his girlfriend had troubles. Though Tommy had only met Destry once, he told Ray the story didn't seem likely since Destry didn't seem like that type of person. That really irritated Ray. His response was more significant than Tommy could possibly have known at the time, without knowledge of Ray's festering jealousy toward Destry. He indignantly told Tommy that in reality, Destry killed himself because he had it too good in life and couldn't handle it. Tommy didn't really think that was a likely reason to shoot yourself, but knew to keep his thoughts to himself.

Tommy left feeling that we weren't what Ray had described and was undoubtedly relieved that it had gone well. Up to that point, nearly six months after his first interview with our detective, he had neither spoken with his parents nor a lawyer about the situation and his potential liabilities, though we didn't know this information at the time. Based on talking to us, friendly folk we were, he probably figured everything was about to go away. As he would soon find out, his assumption couldn't have been further from the truth.

Chapter 18

Based principally upon the evidence developed in the stalking case, in late November of 2005, we filed a malicious prosecution suit against both Ray and Jessie. A layman's definition of malicious prosecution is when someone intentionally, and maliciously, institutes and pursues a legal action that is without probable cause. That certainly applied to what Ray and Jessie did to me when they claimed, without a shred of proof, that I stalked them.

The lawsuit was just a tool to get at the bigger issue, Destry's death. Our lawsuit was big time. Even Ray and Jessie could figure out they would have to get a lawyer and that cost money. In addition to the legal action, we were putting pressure on Ray in other ways.

Brenda was not as concerned with Ray's situation as she was with keeping custody of her three young children, products of her second marriage. Since their divorce, she and her second husband had a contentious relationship when it came to custody issues. Allowing a suspected killer in the house, around the kids, was bad politics and I let her ex-husband know. That was the end of Ray visiting what little family he had left.

The cracks began to show. Ray called my sister, his Aunt Jennifer, to beg for money to get an attorney. Though he had never called before, it didn't seem to bother him that the first time he would display an interest in her life was when he needed money. She told him that we were just trying to get to the bottom of things and that he should understand that. His only comment shook her. Ray stated he didn't know why this was happening to them. After all, they "had never changed their story once since the beginning."

This explanation gave Jennifer a chill down her spine and she called to tell me so. As far as she was concerned, he could have said many things, such as "we didn't do anything" or "we're innocent." Ray saw their innocence as a function of having a consistent story. And besides, they had changed their story since the beginning. He seemed to have forgotten about the phone call and Tommy's involvement, both of which came to light months after Destry died.

Jane, our family friend, also got in touch with us again with another development. After her encounter with Ray and his poetry, she didn't see him anymore. However, she did see him in fall of 2004. While shopping, Jane spotted Ray stocking some shelves. Where most would walk away and hope he didn't see them, that wasn't how Jane lived her life. Speaking her mind was never a problem. She approached Ray and told him to his face that she knew what he had done and he wasn't fooling anyone, then walked away. I like Jane. Most people could take a lesson from her.

It's important to note that Jane never had any sort of relationship with Ray, other than as the mother of one of the many girls he went after in high school. Why he had sought her out in the first place back in 2003 has never been entirely clear, except for this one fact. Ray relates to women, especially mother types, presumably because he felt he never really had one. He wanted a mommy. Jane was the epitome of the mother type. She didn't know Ray before he went after her daughter and only saw him that one more time after his obsession with her played out.

A little over a year later she had another encounter that was much more chilling. One night in late November of 2005, just days after Ray was served with our legal action notifying him of the malicious prosecution suit, Jane was cooking dinner when she heard the front door to her house open. When no one appeared immediately, she went, spatula in hand, to investigate. As she rounded the corner to the front door, she saw Ray standing in her foyer.

True to form, he didn't knock or wait to be invited in. Though she was afraid of Ray, Jane was no femme fatale and she didn't hesitate to exercise her territorial imperative. She yelled at Ray to get out of her house and shooed him out the door with her weapon of opportunity, a spatula. He left.

She didn't give him a chance to get out a word. Whether he was coming to plead for money or to spill his guts to her, we'll never know. More likely, he was looking for support from the only woman he knew and, at least in his mind, had left. Her fear of Ray wasn't unfounded. The experience Jane's daughter had with Ray was so unnerving that to this day, her daughter shakes when talking about him. She knew the real Ray Jones. In fact, after her experiences with Ray in high school, her immediate reaction to news of Destry's death, someone she knew well through years together in band, was "Oh, my god! What has Ray done now?"

That was just hours after his death. She wasn't the only one that had that reaction. In the days after Destry died, we had over a dozen visitors recount to us their reaction to the news. Initially, they believed they were getting the wrong information. When the story of Jim and Janice Allen's grandson committing suicide made the rounds, the response was the same. Surely, it was Ray that had committed suicide, not Destry. Months later, when discussing Destry's mysterious death with friends and acquaintances, the reaction to news that Ray could have been involved drew the same unanimous response. To a person, the words were the same: "Now I understand."

Chapter 19

Come January, 2006, nothing had changed. We were slowly working toward depositions from Ray, Jessie, and Tommy in our malicious prosecution case. When Tommy stopped by in November, the lawsuit hadn't been filed yet and he didn't realize he would be deposed. He thought he was done with it. After the lawsuit was officially filed, our lawyer began pestering him regularly. During these interviews, Tommy was a nervous mess. One of the lawyer's assistants that visited him during this time stated she felt he was going to break into tears at any moment or pee his pants. He was visibly shaking. Tommy was starting to realize that he was in it, whatever it was, up to his eyeballs.

During much of the investigation, we had been researching the owners of various cell phones that were used in conjunction with either Destry's or Jessie's cell phones that night. This doesn't sound so hard, but in an era of divorced households, the person that owns the phone is many times not the name of the person using the phone. In addition, kids borrow other kids' phones to make calls. Nonetheless, slowly but surely we were developing a call log for both Destry and Jessie.

Two of the phone calls on Jessie's phone had been giving us trouble for months. It was one number that called Jessie's phone at two different times. One occurred at about 11 p.m. that night, and the second at 1:30 a.m., about the time we believed Destry was shot. Our detective had finally tracked down the owner of the number and some background on the family, but the name wasn't familiar. Late in January, our lawyer, Chris, and his assistant set out to track down the owner of the phone.

The address was in Marquette, about twenty miles south and a little west of Salina. When they got there, the postmaster told them the address wasn't actually in the town. They headed west toward the open prairie with a vague notion of where they were going. Just as they figured they were probably lost, the house they were looking for appeared. They pulled in and were greeted by a gentleman in the driveway.

Chris and his assistant introduced themselves and informed the guy they were trying to locate the owner of a cell phone listed at his address. He was more than happy to help and, not immediately familiar with the number off the top of his head, went inside to look at his list. Initially, he believed it was his son's. He had at least a couple of kids. He referred to his phone list and remarked that it wasn't his son's, but it appeared to be his stepson's, Tommy.

I wasn't there, but as it was related to me later, it was reminiscent of a moment out of a whodunit on television. Chris remarked, "Tommy L.?" With a querying look on his face, the guy affirmed that was who he was referring to. Why? Chris informed him of the state of affairs concerning Tommy, that he was at the center of homicide investigation and had been for over six months. The color literally drained from his face. Chris told me he seriously feared the guy was going to faint.

The true gravity of the situation was far from lost on the guy, hence the physical symptoms of distress. Unlike most I know, he seemed to grasp the fact homicide wasn't some abstract notion created for entertainment on television. He disclosed this information was all new to him and he was a little miffed Tommy hadn't mentioned it, especially given that he had been home that last weekend.

This was a huge discovery. For nearly eleven months, Ray, Jessie, and Tommy had all along stuck with the story they were together from 9 p.m. until 3 a.m. that night. Just "sittin' and chillin'." But according to phone records, Tommy called them at around 11 p.m. and then again at nearly 1:30 a.m. Why would he need to call someone he was supposedly sitting with from 9 p.m. until 3 a.m.? Why would Ray and Jessie perjure themselves and Tommy lie for them? They weren't really even friends. The only reason they were even hanging out together was because Adam had been a common thread and Tommy was desperate for company on the night of his birthday. Whatever the case, Ray must have been pretty sure whatever happened to Destry occurred before 3 a.m., otherwise his alibi would be worthless.

Tommy's deposition was only a few weeks away, in the middle of February. There was no doubt in my mind he got a phone call from his parents after Chris' visit, so he was aware of what had transpired and how we had knowledge of his phone calls. I suspected his memory of specific details offered up in our chat during his visit to our house would fade, especially after speaking with a lawyer. I don't know that he spoke with an attorney, but if he was my son, I sure as hell would have had him consult one.

Regardless of what he would recall about what was said at our house, I had four witnesses, in addition to myself, that definitely remembered. I wasn't so concerned about his recollection of our past conversation. I was looking forward to his revelations regarding the recently discovered phone calls.

Up to this point, there had been plenty of opportunities, more than a half dozen different conversations, for Tommy to bring up the subject, yet he never did. It was pretty clear when he arrived at the deposition he had finally grasped the dire nature of his situation. He wasn't the carefree kid that stopped by our house the fall before. He looked rather haggard and his body language suggested he was carrying the weight of the world. He didn't smile.

He realized the jig was up concerning the phone calls and, to his credit, didn't attempt to debate the issue. Yes, he had made the phone calls. It was his birthday and he was bummed out nobody seemed to remember. Additionally, there were some family issues weighing on him. He knew Ray and Jessie had been spending a lot of time at Adam's Cross, so he called them around 11p.m. They weren't a first choice, or even a second, but anything was better than being alone.

Tommy was quick to distance himself from Ray and Jessie by pointing out he wasn't even really friends with them and hadn't seen them in months. He had known Jessie since grade school but had nothing to add except that she had buck teeth. He'd only known Ray since Adam died, barely three months. He didn't really know him at all other than through Jessie and the three of them wouldn't have even been together at all if it wasn't for Adam's death.

Tommy brought some Jack Daniels and beer with him to the little get together. He professed to only drinking three to four cans of beer, but Jessie and Ray, in particular, were fond of the Jack Daniels and drank all of the bottle. He didn't remember seeing Destry and Nichole drive by in their vehicles a little after midnight.

The phone call at 1:30 a.m. came up. He had left the party around 1a.m. he thought. Unfortunately, Tommy claimed had no recollection of the call, but he had a theory. Coincidentally, it was the same theory as Jessie's. He had been prone to drinking a lot at that time in his life and there was a good chance that he was simply calling Jessie to assure her he got home alright. If nothing else, Tommy would have us believe he was a thoughtful, conscientious drunk, even after only drinking three or four beers in a little less than two hours, hardly anything by beer drinking standards. He didn't even remember going home.

The real question was, of course, why did he lie about being with them for over six hours. According to Tommy, at first, since he didn't really remember the times, he thought he was just doing them a favor. He didn't really remember that well and was only giving the answers Ray told him to. It didn't seem like that big of a deal. From his perspective, and after listening to

Ray, the world was unfairly out to get Ray and he felt sorry for him.

Tommy was actually pretty righteous about the whole situation at the time. He had agreed with them before the stalking hearing that they would bring his name into the picture. People just needed to leave Ray alone so he could get on with his life. Naively, Tommy just figured we would all believe he was with them and would go away.

However, after our detective visited Tommy at work and encouraged him to approach Ray about coming forth and clearing up the matter, things quickly went downhill in their relationship. When Tommy spoke to Ray and Jessie about the meeting, they went ballistic and accused him of stabbing them in the back. The whole reaction took Tommy by surprise. It wasn't as though he had sought us out and from his perspective, that of a rational person, what our detective proposed wasn't that outrageous. All of a sudden, they didn't seem so much like the desperate, wronged-by-society friends they had portrayed themselves to be. Tommy quickly realized he was being used by people he didn't even really know.

During the three months after Adam's death, he had partied with them, and others, a number of times at the cross. He stated that Ray and Jessie had a tempestuous relationship, often arguing violently. Tommy stated he was personally afraid of him, mostly because if what we were contending was true, he felt he would be in danger. Given Tommy's demeanor, he seemed to believe us.

That was the reason why Tommy, within weeks of speaking with our detective, packed up and moved out of Salina. The last thing Tommy and Ray spoke about, according to Tommy, was that Ray had no use for Tommy if he wasn't going to lie for him. They hadn't spoken since. As far as our malicious prosecution case went, the reason for the deposition in the first place, Tommy affirmed that, judging by what Ray had told him of the situation, he felt Ray was definitely trying to discredit me.

As the deposition ended and Tommy left the room, I wished him luck with school, to which he replied he was leaving the state and heading to Colorado to live. One would think that now he'd come clean about the situation, Tommy would feel better. He didn't look better. He seemed worried and was running away.

As a side note, a couple of years after his deposition I received a phone call from a woman who worked with Tommy's mother. This person related to me that his mother had told everyone in the office Tommy had left the state because his phone had been used that night, he knew what had happened, and feared coming back to Kansas. I thanked my friendly informant for the information and asked if she had related her tale to the SO. She responded she hadn't. I didn't ask why.

When I asked if she had communicated her information to the SO, my purpose wasn't to see if she had followed any sort of proper channel. I was simply attempting to ascertain if this was yet more information the SO hadn't given me. It had been over a year since our attorney had met with the county officials and we had never heard a word from them. Nada. Nothing. I'd already figured out we were on our own and apparently even the general populace of Salina knew it too. Why bother conveying information to people who wouldn't do a thing? Just cut out the middle man and go right to the ones that actually gave a damn and were actually trying to get some justice.

Chapter 20

With Tommy's deposition in the books, the malicious prosecution case against Ray and Jessie was pretty much a done deal, even though we had barely begun. Their own testimony stated they didn't know if I was stalking them or not and had literally no proof I was. Tommy confirmed that in their conversations with him, he felt they were out to discredit me. While appearing to have the case in hand was certainly gratifying and deserved, it wasn't the motivation for our actions. We wanted information. The depositions of Ray and Jessie would be next on the agenda.

Even though we felt strongly we had proven the critical elements necessary to win, the fact was the case was really only just beginning. One of the first stages of a lawsuit is what is referred to as discovery. We were allowed to ask questions of Ray and Jessie that required answering in our effort to get to the bottom of things. In the case of our lawsuit, we were attempting to get to the truth as to whether Ray and Jessie had filed a stalking suit in an effort to discredit me and whatever investigation I was instigating. Should that happen to lead to information that would eventually be useful in our soon to be announced wrongful death lawsuit against Ray and Jessie or for criminal prosecution, so be it. Our questions to them were clearly focused on the long game.

There were only eight questions presented to Ray and Jessie. They ranged from asking about any conversations they had with Destry on the day of his death to if Ray had ever shot the gun and everything in between. It didn't take them much time to answer the questions. They stated they were all irrelevant and, additionally, they asserted their 5th Amendment privileges. The 5th Amendment basically states that a person has the right to not self-incriminate. To be incriminating, disclosures must create a risk of the accused being convicted of the crimes that are revealed. I don't really know, but I'm told under our circumstances this required a meeting in Judge's chambers so the defendants could lay out their case and why they risk being accused if they testified. If immunity is granted, it's because the judge agrees that the totality of circumstances regarding their testimony could serve to be self-incriminating.

Judge Hellmer had been behind the bench for the stalking nonsense, so he had some familiarity with our agenda and the players. Undoubtedly, he was still far from knowledgeable about what was really going on, but did seem to grasp a couple of relevant points. There didn't appear to be any official investigation going on with law enforcement and, regardless of the reason for that, we were pretty blatantly using his court to hunt bear. There wasn't much he could do about it as long as we played by the rules, but he didn't like it.

On one side was an expensive attorney and respectably dressed client and on the other, a couple of clueless children. Additionally, after observing Ray and Jessie on the stand in the stalking matter, and the fact that they were using what in comparison amounted to a court appointed lawyer in the present case, it was hard to tell where this was going to go.

Refusing to answer our questions was pretty simple, but not an option. We requested Judge Hellmer either instruct Ray and Jessie to answer the questions or grant them 5th Amendment protection which would absolve them of the requirement to answer. He did neither.

His reasoning was that if he let them come back into chambers and lay out their case for 5th Amendment protection, they might accidentally tell him they did it. That would be bad from his perspective because he, Judge Hellmer, would then potentially become the star witness in a murder trial and that was something he would rather avoid. We were welcome to appeal his decision, but for the time being Ray and Jessie didn't have to answer the questions and he wasn't going to afford them 5th Amendment protection. Judge Hellmer's conduct was, in itself, a testament to his recognition that Ray and Jessie weren't clever enough for him to take a chance on even talking to them.

Wow. Look up self-serving gutlessness in the dictionary and apparently there is a photo of Judge Jerome Hellmer. However, his refusal to do his job really didn't do anything to impede our malicious prosecution lawsuit. We could still depose Ray and Jessie and get information from them. The only thing really of any significance was the fact that the desire by Saline County officials to do anything remotely resembling assisting in the pursuit of justice on Destry's behalf was non-existent on multiple levels – the SO, the prosecutor, the coroner, and now the judiciary. At another place and time, the judge's ruling would have doubtlessly enraged me, but given what we had gone through with the other elements of Saline County government it was more darkly amusing than it was disturbing.

At least they were all on the same page. Hellmer knew exactly what he was doing. He may have been a symbol of justice and stood for all that was right at one time, I don't really know. If nothing else, he obviously preferred to be the ringmaster in his circus rather than one of the acts. Screw us, our family, and that poor, blindfolded woman with the scales of justice dangling from her hand. After all, a guy's got to watch out for his own butt.

Chapter 21

There are a couple of firm rules for depositions. Tommy had figured it out easily enough. "I don't know" is the best answer and the fewer the words spoken, the better. Ray and Jessie were poor learners it seemed.

Ray's deposition was in April of 2006 and was, for the most part, unremarkable. Mostly, he displayed his inability to process dates. Our questioning was pretty restrained, per Judge Hellmer's instructions, given the focus was the malicious prosecution suit. Plus, Ray had his counsel with him, so expectations of a revelation were pretty low. What we were really trying to do was to continue nailing down the details of our case by getting more testimony from him that I wasn't doing anything remotely close to stalking and that even they knew it. If other things emerged, so be it.

It seemed that in the year since the original stalking case, even Ray had gained some perspective on the situation, though I don't think telling us was necessarily in his best interest. At the time, he had come to realize that if a person really believes someone is responsible for the death of their child, they might seek revenge. I don't personally know why it took so long for this to occur to Ray, other than it suggests just how far from normal he was. The more he thought about it, the more he convinced himself of this heretofore unseen danger. All of a sudden, my driving by his house on the way to school or work were clearly threatening activities, even though it had been going on for quite some time. I was everywhere, at least in his imagination.

The one point in the deposition of particular interest to me was Ray's rendition of what occurred when I took him out to the Depot a week after Destry's death. His version of the evening had been evolving ever since that night. According to him, I took him out there specifically to accuse him of killing Destry. At one point, I grabbed his arms and shook him, beseeching him to come clean. At another interview a few months later, the story included me forcing him to look at photos of the scene so, in his words, "I could admire my handiwork." He elaborated on how, when he ran into the night, the one point we both seem to agree on, I pursued him, yelling for him to come back and how sorry I was for accusing him. Sobbing, I stumbled upon him in the dark and hugged him "like a linebacker" as he described it. He did what he could to comfort me. And, oh yeah, he did tell me about the phone call to Destry that same night.

Good lord. What an imagination. Why not just say nothing happened at all, deny the entire event? After all, there were no witnesses to our conversation. In order to buy what he is saying, one thing has to be taken for granted – one big thing. If a person follows the thread of logic in the story, there is a significant problem for what I would term normal people. According to him, I took him out to the Depot to accuse him and, ultimately, profusely apologized, in tears to boot, for unjustly suspecting him of murder. All he had to do was declare emotionally he knew nothing about the evening, didn't kill Destry, and I was good to go.

Really? I ask the reader, if you seriously suspected someone of murdering your child, planned to confront them, and did, would their simple protestation they didn't do it really suffice? Obviously not. But in Ray's version of events, after he calmed me down, I drove us back to town, my suspicions relieved by his reassurances.

Unfortunately for Ray, he always has to include details so his fabrications have a little meat to them. The story he fed to Sharon on the first anniversary of the rafting accident is a good example. Who's to know, after all? The listener wasn't there. But some things are verifiable that he forgets about. For instance, when he told an acquaintance I forced him to look at the photos of the scene, it was a very shocking and colorful detail that really made the story. Now, I could simply declare I didn't show him anything, but it would just be his word against mine. Who to believe?

Well, one detail makes the decision pretty easy. I didn't even have the photos in my possession until two months *after* our meeting at the Depot. This is a quantifiable, concrete fact. In addition, why would I show them to Ray, even if I did have them? Theoretically, the killer was one of the few that would know the details of the scene. Therefore, if Ray knew details of the scene, it meant he had been there. I certainly wouldn't give those to him.

The fact Ray was lying about this wasn't as disturbing as the fact he could describe the scene, declaring the gore wasn't something that would bother a deer hunter. Since he had hunted deer, he presumably would know. Bear in mind, this was his cousin he was talking about, not some poor schmuck on a crime show with the face blurred out. Ray was all man. So the question is really this. How did he know what the crime scene looked like without ever having seen photos?

Jessie's deposition, in early June of 2006, was far more productive. She seemed to have a marginally better grasp of the English language and stayed relatively consistent when asked about the stalking hearing and her testimony. She was her predictable in-your-face defiant self. Nothing new emerged relating to the stalking case itself, but when asked who her friends were lately, she gave the name of one Sandy.

Jessie had always been a hard worker, having two jobs at the same time when she and Ray first got together. But over time, she began letting Ray dominate her life and priorities. He fed her bitterness toward the world and had Jessie convinced she was being pursued. Eventually, she quit both jobs, sold her car, and stayed at home, even though they had little cash flow. Allowing Jessie to be out around others might contaminate her with a different perspective on life than the one he envisioned for her. She was, for all practical purposes, isolated from the world, just the way Ray wanted. That she had found a friend other than Ray wasn't really a surprise. What was a surprise was that she would even give up her name in the first place, given the grief Sandy would bring on them.

Chapter 22

The middle of June, 2006, our detectives, Gerard and Kathern, began looking for Sandy. The name wasn't familiar, but was close to one we had come to know through our investigation. At first, we thought Jessie had simply misstated the name, but when the person we thought she was talking about was contacted, she verified that, indeed, there was a Sandy and it was her sister. The detectives headed straight for her house.

Our investigation was typical of most I think. It's usually a case of three steps forward and two steps back. Dead ends are the norm so when they got to Sandy's house and began asking a few vague questions about Ray, Jessie, and what they had potentially talked with her about in regards to the night Destry died, she didn't have anything new to add. Gerard and Kathern were just getting up to leave and were thanking her for her time when she nonchalantly blurted out something to the effect that Ray and Jessie had been with Destry at the Depot the night he died. It didn't seem to be news as far as she was concerned.

When the detectives, outwardly trying to not react to this bit of news, casually asked about Sandy's statement, she just as casually remarked they told her they had been with him but they wanted to go out and party more. Destry didn't want to go and seemed kind of bummed out, so they left him to find greener partying pastures. Sandy stated Ray and Jessie felt really bad when they heard he had killed himself, since they had left him there knowing he was depressed, but they had been going to counseling and were only one session from being better. Unfortunately, they didn't have the money for that last session.

Gerard and Kathern thanked her for her time and told her they would be back in touch with her. They went back to her house a couple of day's later, affidavit in hand. She reaffirmed her statement and signed the affidavit stating the same. We never told her it was new information for our case and she never asked.

Kathern began to foster a relationship with Sandy over the next few weeks. I think it's important to understand that at the time, Sandy firmly believed Ray and Jessie had nothing to do with Destry's death and defended them enthusiastically as kids that needed time to grow up and make mistakes. Ray and Jessie had become her drinking buddies and the whole thought of death up close and personal freaked her out. That being said, Sandy was more than a little curious.

She wanted to solve the murder and prove that the kids were not involved. Kathern volunteered to Sandy, in what became frequent cell phone calls that she was in the same situation, more or less. She was just trying to find out what had happened to Destry, who was definitely murdered, how Ray and Jessie figured into the whole thing, and was open to all theories.

Kathern also strategically introduced the suggestion that surely Ray, though probably not involved, would want to help find Destry's killer. Maybe he could come up with some ideas we hadn't thought of. Sandy also thought Ray, Destry's cousin, would surely want to help. Sandy agreed she would be the conduit between what we officially knew of the shooting and Ray's theories as to what could have potentially happened. It seemed like a good plan to us, if we could just get Ray on board.

He jumped at the chance. Ray and Jessie quickly realized it was the perfect opportunity to drag my name through the mud some more. They knew full well Sandy was talking to us. The first theory had to do with a large marijuana growing operation I was involved in out at the Depot. I wasn't alone in this endeavor, however. I had a business partner.

As it turned out, Destry had been stealing my pot by the garbage bag and selling it without my knowledge or my partner's knowledge either it turned out. When this became known, Ray speculated that I had refused to make the matter right with my partner, and consequently, Destry was killed to settle a drug debt. Ray stated he could verify at least part of the story because Destry had taken him to the Depot several weeks before he died to see my plants growing in coffee cans. Except when they got to the Depot there weren't any coffee cans or plants to be found.

Very creative and damning at the same time. Now I was apparently a boob ogling, creepy drug dealer who, in actuality, really already knew what happened to my son. He was killed by my drug partner, but rather than seek to even the score with him, I would rather spend a fortune trying to pin it on my nephew. I guess I didn't want to screw up my business arrangement. Where Destry rates on this scale, as my oldest son, is anyone's guess. However, since Ray and Jessie didn't have the faintest idea what parenthood and love are about, it seemed like a workable scenario to them.

Just in case I need to mention it, for the record, I wasn't growing weed. I could spend the better part of a chapter outlining why his assertions are absurd and can be proven so. It makes my head hurt defending myself from idiots and their maniacal ravings. Another one of his theories was that I was having sexual relations with Nichole behind Destry's back, we had a blowup, and I killed Destry over Nichole. Add rapist to my credentials. Presumably I had some reason for trying to pin it on Ray, even though I had seemingly gotten away with it. My motivation? Like I said, it makes my head hurt.

One evening, Sandy agreed with the investigators suggestion that she meet with us at the Depot to discuss possibilities. At that point, we had been feeding Sandy's ego pretty well and she was doing all she could to help, even though in reality she didn't really grasp her true role, which was as the official pot stirrer. While there, we vaguely described the scene and entertained her earnest theories, but at one point, we planted a couple of seeds.

We revealed the information that there was vomit at the scene and we speculated it could have come from the killer becoming sickened at what he had just done. The vomit had never been tested for DNA, so we weren't sure. Additionally, we informed her there was a bowl shaped ashtray full of bullets at the scene we were having trouble understanding, since the weapon was already loaded. Sure enough, she returned home and brought this up to Ray at their next get together.

Having visited the actual crime scene, Sandy felt quite empowered. She was able to discuss the whole thing more knowledgably than before and had questions for Ray. She brought up the vomit, speculating about this and that. Ever the man's man, Ray volunteered the scene wasn't one that would cause a deer hunter to get sick. Sandy stated Ray revealed he had seen the photos when I showed them to him during our visit to the Depot, the same one where I supposedly grabbed Ray's arms and yelled in his face he was the killer. Of note, when asked whether Ray was a deer hunter, Sandy didn't have the faintest idea. If she was making up the part about the deer hunter comment, one would think she would at least affirm Ray was a deer hunter. In fact, he did hunt deer growing up.

Sandy stated Ray was especially interested in the ashtray full of bullets, and repeatedly asked her if we had said where they were located. This was of note because when I first talked with him when he visited in September of 2004, I told him there were empty casings at the scene. He immediately wanted to know where they were found. I didn't mention they were mixed in with the live ammo in the ashtray. In fact, I didn't reveal the part concerning the existence of the bowl of bullets at all.

Something about the ashtray full of ammunition and where they were really interested him. Maybe it was because, in the haste of the moment, he forgot to put them back where they were originally located. We had always wondered why Destry would need ammunition for a gun that he knew was already loaded.

To be clear, Ray wasn't Sandy's friend, Jessie was, but he would always be there with Jessie, unless he was on the road with the company he was working for. Knowing this, Kathern began to push the cheating-on-Jessie angle to Sandy, attempting to undermine Jessie's devotion to Ray. We suspected that Jessie could be just as harmful to Ray's case as helpful if she believed he was the lowlife husband he actually was. It was revealed condoms were found at the scene and possibly they belonged to Ray and his underage girlfriend. We also made sure Sandy was aware of just how sexually involved Ray had been with the girl, of how he had chased her back to Oklahoma when her parents came to get her. She dutifully went and talked to Jessie.

This information had the desired effect and greatly upset Jessie. When Ray got home, he got an earful. Ray called Sandy at her place of employment and told Sandy to keep away from his wife because she just upset Jessie all the time. He also made sure to tell her that he would do whatever he had to in order to protect his wife. Sandy took it as a threat on her life and was shaken. She called Kathern and relayed the information.

It looked like we had played out our hand, but the more Sandy thought about it, the more her fear morphed into anger. How dare that little twit threaten her! She suggested she would set up a meeting with Ray and Jessie and accuse him outright, with the detectives hidden, weapons at the ready, in the next room.

On television, it all looks simple enough. What television fails to ever genuinely get across is the gravity of situations such as the one Sandy was suggesting. After finding myself confronted with my cold, bloodied, dead son, combined with the real life experiences of the detectives, the reality of what Sandy was proposing certainly wasn't lost on us. We told Sandy no way we would put her in a position like that and backed completely away from the whole thing.

Chapter 23

Toward the end of July, I suggested to Kathern and Gerard that they pay Sharon, down at the *Salina Journal*, a visit, since technically she could potentially have information about Ray and Jessie. She had, after all, been the one to write the *A Life Reclaimed* article about Ray and had attempted to speak with them in regards to our investigation. I didn't really think she had anything to add and, given her profession, would likely be guarded with any answers provided. I hadn't been in contact with the newspaper in any way since their original interest in the story nearly a year before, which had apparently waned. I didn't think it could hurt to revisit the situation.

As suspected, Sharon had nothing to reveal, but was interested in the fact the investigation was still going on. Apparently, the newspaper felt I was either deluded or lacked determination when we had talked the year before and figured the story would just go away. Plus, they were just ticking off the SO, which probably wasn't good for business.

Most believe our newspaper somehow or another represents the interests of the citizens of Salina, which might be true in some instances, but only as long as those interests coincide with corporate interests. Their job is to make money and report the news, in that order. I personally have no problem with that, but I don't believe most people understand their priorities. Put another way, is it likely a newspaper would report on a story that, if reported on, could well result in the loss of profits?

When Sharon inquired as to the state of the investigation and if it was still ongoing, Kathern and Gerard enthusiastically affirmed it was alive and well. They let her know that, in fact, there was a herd of lawyers involved and the whole thing was about to blow wide open. They thanked her for her time and left.

Within a few days, Sharon was in touch with us. She needed to bring the photographer out to the Depot for new photos since the ones from the year before were taken when there were no leaves on the trees and now it was August, a greener time of year. As the date neared for the story to be published, Sharon met with me so I could proofread the story. After all, I was basically their only source of information. For all they knew, I had a creative writing streak. If it wasn't for the SO and the coroner refusing to cooperate with her, I'm sure they would have written me off as a lunatic, or at least a lunatic with no proof.

I found their desire for me to look over the story before publication interesting. In my experience, newspaper articles many times inadvertently contain mistakes and misquote that can come as a surprise both to the interviewee and to the general readers. But for us to actually see how our interview turned out before it went to press was new. I literally read the entire article as it was to appear and was asked for my input on accuracy. Apparently, pointing at me after the fact if everything went to hell had some therapeutic value for them. I affirmed they had it right and it went to press.

On Wednesday, August 16, 2006, the story ran with the following headline: *Murder or suicide: How did Destry Die?*, accompanied by a photo of Destry. It was the lead story on the front page and continued on to page three where it took up the entire page, not a single advertisement. They hadn't changed it a bit since I had proofed it.

The SO repeatedly had no comment. The prosecutor repeatedly had no comment. The coroner had no comment. It was, after all, over two years and two months and still an open case. Why? No comment. Ray and Jessie had no comment. The departments involved had broken their own internal rules, by their own admission. Mike Smith, the lead investigator, hadn't even looked at the cell phone records until nearly a week after the death. Details were omitted, lies told. It went on and on. The article made clear it was far from a simple suicide and, most importantly, nobody wanted to talk about their role in it. Period.

The ostrich approach. Stick your head in the ground long enough and the problem will go away. There is, of course, another way to look at it. It's an ostrich standing still with its throat near the ground. Sooner or later, a predator will come along. Thank goodness I'm a patient man. The last paragraph of the article made our intentions clear.

"This isn't about Destry, per se. We would like to catch the person who killed Destry, but that might not be possible. We're looking at the bigger picture. Somebody needs to clean up the sheriff's office, the police department, and the county attorney's office, and make them do their jobs. We just don't think people ought to have to go through this."

One interesting event transpired soon after the article came out. A good friend of Theresa's, Shelley, someone that had known Destry since he was born, was a staunch and reliable ally in the fight to find the truth. In her quest, she contacted a local radio program and suggested they do a show about our plight. It really wasn't their cup of tea. The show typically addressed light, local topics, such as whether citizens should be allowed to park recreational vehicles in their driveways. Homicide, cover ups, and violations of civil rights were certainly out of their league. Nonetheless, they visited the house and spoke with us.

Clark Sanders, a local radio personality and lead on the show, was known as an opinionated conservative and his partner, Nancy, was the opposite. It made for light hearted, often times goofy banter first thing in the morning. Clark, who considered himself a true patriot, simply couldn't believe that law enforcement would do anything wrong. The concept of self preservation seemed to be a foreign concept to the man. Anyway, he must've called someone at the SO because, within two days, on a hot and sticky Sunday afternoon, Investigator Smith showed up at Shelley's house.

He found her working in the yard. Since the debacle, according to a source that worked at the newspaper, Smith had been transferred to road patrol, a seeming demotion. During one of his patrols in the county, he took the occasion to stop by and talk to Shelley. Smith appeared casual as he stated he had information that indicated she might know something about Destry Allen's death. Obviously, Shelley had no idea what he was talking about and was silently wondering why he would assume such a thing out of the blue.

Smith spent over two hours talking with her. He had a couple of objectives. His original question was really just a pretext to break the ice. Mostly, he spent his time trying to get Shelley to speak with us about dropping our investigation. It seemed everyone down at the SO felt bad we were being duped by our detectives and lawyers into thinking there was something where there wasn't. Popular opinion was that these parasites just wanted our money and they, the boys down at the SO, felt simply terrible about it. Quite a compassionate bunch.

Smith also had quite a few questions about why everyone that knew Destry didn't buy the suicide story. He wanted to know what kind of kid he was. At least, that's how he wanted the questions to sound. What he really wanted to know was what we knew. What had our investigation turned up? Shelley wanted to know why he was talking with her. Why not approach us directly? Smith's answer made no sense. He replied they couldn't come talk to us because of the lawsuits we had against Ray. What this had to do with anything was a mystery. If simply being in a lawsuit would keep cops away, there'd be even more lawsuits than there already are. It was just an excuse for avoiding us.

Who knew how long this would have gone on, except Smith got on the subject of how he had done such a thorough and splendid job. He was completely confident he had done everything by the book and come to the correct conclusion, even though he admitted Destry's death was one of the first he had worked. His only mistake, as far as he was concerned, was he didn't measure the distance from Destry's head to a wall or some other such insignificant detail. As a comment on Smith's investigative abilities, the floor was covered with one square foot tiles. Five tiles equals five feet. Determining the distance anywhere in the room was simply a matter of counting the tiles in the photos.

The heat and mosquitoes of the afternoon were wearing on Shelley and even though she professed to some enjoyment subjecting Smith to the conditions, she was tiring of him and his idiotic air of superiority. She asked him if he was such an expert, did he realize he didn't even know if the gun found at the scene was the one that shot Destry, since they had never retrieved the bullet from his head. How did he even know the ballistics matched? Had he ever thought of that? According to Shelley, the look on his face said it all. He should definitely watch more CSI. Smith left pretty soon after that.

Why did he visit Shelley? Was Smith showing some sort of misguided initiative on his own part or did his boss, Sheriff Kochanowski, ask him to do it? Did he really think it was that easy to stop our investigation? I'm sure they wanted to know what was going on. What if our investigation resulted in some sort of revelation? What if we got Ray to confess? That would've been pretty embarrassing. They didn't even call to interview him about his role that night, probably for the same reason. That's why they didn't approach us. They didn't want the information to potentially pursue a case for fear it might mean they would actually have to do something and reveal their ineptness and corruption. They just wanted to know if they were going to have to eat crow anytime soon and if they could do anything about it.

Chapter 24

Dr. Charles Allred

Dr. Charles Allred is a family physician in Salina, Kansas, who also serves as the coroner for Saline County and has since 1998. The Saline County Commissioners gave him the task of finding a full-time coroner, but until that time, he would fill the void. I'm not sure what the pay currently is, but in January of 2007, a slight raise was approved that put it at $2,400 per month, plus $100 per call. At around one hundred calls per year, the job pays in the neighborhood of $39,000 per year. That equates to about $100 per hour for eight hours a week, fifty weeks a year. I'm no doctor, but it seems like pretty good pay for a part-time gig that basically requires no expertise.

Allred couldn't find any takers at the time and still can't, so he's stuck with the job. The county commissioners don't really seem to care since they have him on the hook. The fact he openly doesn't want the job, is blatantly contemptuous, arrogant, and, according to one ex-board member from the local hospital, is considered a buffoon by many, doesn't seem to enter into the county's decision making process.

Allred doesn't even go out on all of the calls. In those situations, a deputy coroner is dispatched, of which Saline County had eight in 2007. In Kansas, a physician is required to fill the post. Forensic pathology knowledge and skills aren't required. In fact, in some areas of the country with super low population densities, I've been told that veterinarians are used to fill the post. This may sound surprising, but the position doesn't really require any more expertise than an observant, intelligent, life-long hunter would possess.

Most deaths are pretty cut and dried, really. A lot of old people dying in the middle of the night, auto accidents, and the like. When there is any question whatsoever, or in certain pre-defined situations, Kansas Bureau of Investigation (KBI) is called and they take over. It's as simple as that. The only expertise required is being able to dial a phone number, a skill Allred apparently has never mastered.

The fact Allred has only taken one mandatory two-day class when he took the job demonstrates both the fact that not a lot is expected from a coroner and the fact that Allred, as a professional, has no desire to perform his job at a more competent level, even if not technically required. For instance, he literally has no qualifications in blood spatter analysis, crime scene analysis, gunshot entry/exit wounds, or any other field of forensic expertise. Yet, in our case, he decided in just a few minutes that it was, in his words, a "pristine suicide" and wrote a report attributing Destry's death to breaking up with his girlfriend the night before. Romeo and Juliet come to life. There was no evidence that Destry and Nichole had broken up and it wasn't written in any report, but to Allred, it fit his love gone wrong fantasy perfectly and he wrote it down as a fact.

Allred documents additional proof of his incompetence in his report. Nowhere does he list that Destry, though shot in the brain, actually likely suffocated from pulmonary edema, as evidenced by the foam covering his nose and mouth when I found him. The condition is a common result of brain trauma. Though it may seem obvious, dead people don't bleed, or breathe for that matter.

In practical terms, what this means is if you are shot and die instantaneously, there will be very little blood at the scene, or breathing to cause the edema foam. Unless a heart is beating, breathing and bleeding don't occur. Additionally, he lists the time of death as two different times, two hours apart, in separate reports. One states it was around 2 a.m. and the other 4 a.m.

In fact, Allred doesn't even seem to know what the foam was or what it was indicative of. On the death certificate, he states Destry died in one to two minutes. Pulmonary edema occurs when excess fluid accumulates in the lungs. This occurs because fluid is filtered into the lungs faster than it can be removed. Basically, the victim drowns. It certainly takes more than one to two minutes, as does bleeding the voluminous amount found at the scene.

Allred has even testified in court that, at times, he doesn't read the law enforcement reports which accompany the deaths he signs off on. He certainly didn't in our case. Whether they contradict his conclusions is of no concern to him. After all, he is a very important man and what he thinks is all that matters. Just ask him.

Sadly, Allred suffers from "I am doctor, ergo I am God" syndrome. The fact of the matter is someone is needed to sign the death certificates, and since Allred is breathing and can't get out of the job, he qualifies. If he lets a killer get away every now and again, so what? It likely wasn't the first time. He doesn't cost much and fits the bill. He couldn't lose the position if he tried and since he doesn't even want the damn job, he has little incentive to do it correctly or professionally.

In our case, Allred broke the law, helping a killer to go free. When we made the county commissioners aware in January of 2007, their only reaction was "What do you want us to do? Nobody wants the job." The commissioners consisted of Craig Stephenson, Sherri Barragree, and the most recent addition, Randy Duncan. Stephenson, the most consistently obnoxious of the bunch, volunteered he had already spoken with Sheriff Kochanowski about the matter, as if he would have had anything relevant to add.

He and Barragree had a history of trying to shove issues down voter's throats, regardless of what the voters wanted and, in general, they had a pretty high opinion of themselves and their expertise in county matters. In Duncan's defense, apparently still a member of humanity and clearly grasping the gravity of the situation, he seemed pretty concerned with what we were alleging and even questioned if they had to extend the contract immediately. Barragree and Stephenson just looked at him like he was an idiot and said yes, even though they had eight deputy coroners, it had to be done. Then they gave Allred a raise and extended his contract.

You have to say one thing for Saline County. Its employees, at least the ones we've dealt with, are consistently arrogant, corrupt, and incompetent when it comes to representing the best interests of the residents. Fortunately, Stephenson and Barragree paid when the voters booted them out in the next election.

Finding a seventeen-year-old shot nearly between the eyes that, additionally, died an unattended death would unquestionably qualify for an autopsy anywhere in the U.S.A., except for Saline County, Kansas. KBI told us they, as an organization, had never heard of not conducting an autopsy on a minor, period, much less one shot in the head, unattended.

This brings up what is probably one of the most telling details of Destry's case. When he was at the scene that day, Allred spoke with my dad, uttering the infamous pristine suicide phrase. He began talking about the disposition of the body when my dad interrupted him and stated straight out Allred was talking to the wrong person that he needed to talk with the parents. Allred told my dad there was nothing to talk about, period. State law dictated an autopsy would take place and we had no say in the next step.

Yet when my father and I visited the SO not five hours later, the lead investigator, Mike Smith, told us though it was state law, they were not going to perform an autopsy, but we were welcome to have one performed ourselves. It wasn't a question I was really prepared for. I remember thinking while sitting in his office they must be awfully sure if they're willing to admittedly break the law. That definitely influenced my decision to not have one done on our own behalf, since the cops were consciously breaking the law due to their certainty.

A representative from the funeral home called Allred's office numerous times in the next two days to arrange for the funeral, but it wasn't until Saturday morning he released the body, forty-eight hours after I found Destry. The representative basically asked him what the hell was going on. The family needed the body. Why weren't they releasing it? As related to me, Allred seemed to be uncertain what to do and finally, after being pressed for a decision, decided to release Destry's body.

All of the other actions in this case could conceivably be explained by the fact the authorities in Saline County are profoundly heartless and dangerously corrupt. When looked at the case in totality, it doesn't seem very likely, but nonetheless conceivable. Allred's actions are the ones that stand alone in that he completely contradicted himself, broke the law, and judging by his demeanor when the funeral home called to take possession of the body, he knew it.

To this day, Allred stands by his actions, declaring that in his opinion it's completely up to the coroner to decide when an autopsy should be done on a child, totally contrary to published law and professional opinion. As he stated in an article in the newspaper, in his opinion he can do whatever he wants. Try that one on the officer next time you get pulled over, that the speed limit is open to interpretation and, in your opinion, you can drive as fast as you want.

Allred won't even admit he screwed up when he didn't have an autopsy performed on Destry. After all, as everyone knows, gods can do nothing wrong. I personally find his reasoning disturbingly criminal in its rational. According to most of the guys in prison, they didn't actually do anything wrong either.

So the big question is this. What happened between the time Allred visited the scene and forty-eight hours later that made him change his mind, or even five hours later, since Smith explicitly indicated an autopsy wasn't going to be done when my dad and I met with him that same afternoon? Why did he go from being emphatic an autopsy had to be done because of state law to just keeping the body on ice for two days until pressed by the funeral home to make a decision? All he had to do was call KBI and his role was over. In fact, it would have been expected from him.

Certainly, the simplest explanation is that he was a good soldier and did what he was ordered to do. The powers that be were going to teach us what happens to people that rock the boat in their fetid, little cesspool. Destry was a problem that, obligingly, went away. Good riddance. The county didn't need residents like him, demanding law abiding officials and justice. What the hell was he thinking about? His death likely saved Chief Hill's job, Saline County Prosecutor Ellen Mitchell's job, and the county itself was saved from embarrassment, in addition to potentially paying out a huge settlement. As the saying goes, don't look a gift horse in the mouth, and they didn't.

Chapter 25

Sheriff Glen Kochanowski

Sheriff Glen Kochanowski has served as the Saline County Sheriff since 1996 after retiring from the SPD. In between the two jobs, he served, in effect, as an interim police chief for SPD for several years. At nearly sixteen years, he is the longest serving sheriff in Saline County history. Kochanowski is an affable enough guy and for years I had a certain respect for him, based principally upon one incident.

At the business I worked for, we had been having break-ins and though the perpetrator never got more than petty cash, he wouldn't stop. This ultimately resulted in the cash drawer being wired to an alarm that contacted SPD when triggered. One night during Kochanowski's tenure as police chief, the thief broke in, tried to open the cash drawer, and set off the alarm. SPD responded and then called the personnel director from our company, since they couldn't actually enter the building without a key. When he arrived, the officers on the scene were kind of pissy and seemed to think it was a false alarm as they couldn't find any problems. By the front door, there was a tall bush and as the officers were explaining the situation, it was pointed out to them by the employee the window was broken out. All of a sudden the guns came flying out.

They entered to find a crowbar on the cabinet and a plant stand knocked over in the hallway going to the back of the offices. It appeared someone had left in a hurry. An exit from the offices at the back went directly into the poorly lit and shadowy storage and production warehouse. At the back of the warehouse was a motorized garage door. After a pathetic effort at searching the grounds and an excuse the canine guy was on vacation that week, the cops left. Besides, they rationalized, the guy had probably opened up the garage door at the back and left.

When all of this was relayed to me the next morning, I asked if the door was left open when the thief left. No, it was closed. I immediately questioned why in the world a guy that clearly knows the cops are outside and running for his life would stop to close the door behind him? I went directly to the door and sure enough, lying on the ground was the main door lock, where it had been taken apart by a screwdriver after the cops left. The thief obviously didn't know he could push the button located by his shoulder to open the garage door, which was located right next to the main door. Also obvious was the fact the SPD had their man cornered and let him go because they were lazy. The perpetrator was never caught, but after the close call, also never came back.

The next day, after the facts I discovered were relayed to SPD, an unmarked Crown Victoria arrived, slowly cruised the grounds, and then the occupants came inside. One of those occupants was Chief Kochanowski. After a quick review of the facts with the president of our company, myself in the back of the room, Kochanowski actually said the right thing.

He threw his officers under the bus. He stated he had idiots working for him. One of them was more worried about the fact he tore his pants climbing the fence, and another unit was parked nearly a quarter of a mile behind the facility rendering them useless. A platoon could have walked out the back and they wouldn't have been able to see them. He apologized profusely and left. It was refreshingly honest.

So, whatever became of that man? In the case just cited, he was certainly willing to admit mistakes were made and even went so far as to apologize for a measly offense with no real victims. Yet in our case, he went out of his way to perpetrate a cover-up of monumental proportions to avoid admitting the obvious. He still has at least a few idiots working for him, as well as compatriots with him, and they screwed up on an unimaginable scale.

Though it's hard to believe, apparently leaving a legacy of the worst incompetence, unaccountability, negligence, and corruption in Saline County law enforcement history works for Kochanowski.

At one point in the investigation, our lawyer requested the .22 revolver so we could analyze it ourselves. He tried in vain to call Kochanowski, until one day he didn't give a name to the receptionist. Not knowing it was Chris, he answered the phone this time. He took a defensive position from the first word of the conversation. We just wanted to know if we could do our own tests on the gun since they were done with it. Kochanowski said it wasn't going to happen. He stated that as long as we were asserting there was a cover-up, he would never release the gun.

So, in other words, as long as we were asserting there was a cover-up, he was going to perpetrate a cover-up. Brilliant strategy. It was like he got his ideas from Ray's own play book. Chris wrote clarifying that technically, we hadn't been alleging a cover-up. We were simply saying they were incompetent idiots.

What was particularly disturbing about the encounter was the fact Kochanowski was depending upon the unofficial SO psychic for his information. Most aren't aware there is one and, quite frankly, I wasn't sure either until the misinformation we filled her with came spilling out of Kochanowski's own mouth.

Keely's name had come up during the investigation and when we found her, she claimed to be the department's psychic and worked with Investigator Smith, the guy that was the point man in our own debacle. She told us they were even drinking buddies and that it irritated Smith's wife. I didn't know about her psychic abilities and didn't care at the time. The fact was, she was a direct line to the SO, at least according to her.

Knowing this, we let her visit the Depot under the pretense of giving us her psychic impressions. While we had her there, we told her we thought maybe the cops themselves were involved in Destry's death, possibly on orders from other interested parties, and were covering it all up. It was a ludicrous assertion, but harmless since she wasn't really a player. Or so we thought until the accusation came out of Kochanowski.

It turns out the Saline County Sheriff uses a secret psychic for a source of what he considers unimpeachable information. I'm no legal scholar, but maybe looking at the various court transcripts we created in our case, where potential suspects perjure themselves and know details they shouldn't, would be a better source of information. It's common knowledge in legal circles that civil cases often times develop information that can be used in criminal cases, but it's useless if law enforcement doesn't give a damn.

Under the heading of "There's more than one way to skin a cat," I ran for Saline County Sheriff in 2008. Kochanowski was running unopposed, which I found viscerally unacceptable. I quickly switched parties, becoming a Democrat, and filed. The filing date happened to be the anniversary of the day Destry died, June 10. It seemed a small token from Karma.

My statement on the front page was simple and direct. My qualifications were that I knew right from wrong and good from bad, something our current sheriff didn't know the meaning of. Additionally, he was incompetent and unaccountable. It was a satisfying opening salvo. My ads featured a photo of myself with the statement, "Because our children matter."

As I have repeatedly stated, nobody ever got in touch with us after we met with the authorities in December of 2004. Ultimately, we spent nearly $150,000 on our investigation but could never get anyone's attention to any meaningful degree. Now, for only a thousand dollar filing fee, Kochanowski would be forced to stand before me. It seemed like a bargain. As expected, he made excuses, mixed with a choice lie or two.

At the time, my goal wasn't to be sheriff so much as make the residents of Saline County aware of what their officials were up to and keep them from doing it again. Additionally, I had a certain curiosity about how the residents felt. For anyone paying attention, the election was a direct referendum on if Saline County residents thought it was acceptable for law enforcement officials to violate civil rights, cover up the murder of children, and assist their killers in getting away. Not a person was saying what I was alleging wasn't true, not even Kochanowski. He simply refused to talk about it, as it was still an open case.

In a radio interview about a week before the election with both of us present, Kochanowski took the opportunity to assure me that changes had been made down at the department and things were better now. Such a gracious guy. Of course, he couldn't call us to tell us that. I had to corner him in a room about the size of a small bathroom to even get that admission, and we had to be on the air.

He also asserted they had done an investigation. I told the listeners he was a liar and that the only investigation done was by me and my wife. I also made the assertion that KBI felt Saline County law enforcement was the worst in Kansas. Up to that point, Kochanowski's strategy of just keeping his mouth shut had been working pretty well, but that statement was too much for him. I knew it would be.

In another interview that evening sponsored by the League of Women Voters and local media, I again made the assertion. He bit like a big, fat carp. Kochanowski stated he had called KBI after I had made the assertion that morning and they had assured him they weren't the worst in the state. Hardly a ringing endorsement. Though it sounds better than being the worst, it's not much better. Following his line of logic then, was I making it up? Was I, the father of the dead kid, a liar? Quickly realizing his conundrum, he spit out a quick lie in an attempt to deflect responsibility and pass the buck.

Kochanowski stated for the benefit of the audience that he didn't know why an autopsy hadn't been done. They had ordered one but it didn't happen. A huge lie, but who in the audience would know? If nothing else, it affirmed the basis of my election campaign. He was an incompetent and unaccountable leader. I'm pretty sure admitting you ordered something to be done, knowing it wasn't done, and you didn't do anything about it is the definition of incompetent and unaccountable. He was the sheriff, for god's sake.

There was some obvious focus on the fact I had no law enforcement experience, though the only requirement to run for sheriff in Kansas is possessing a GED. Having two college degrees probably over qualifies me for the position. This may seem illogical, but the fact is the post is a political, figurehead position elected by the citizens, who deserve and expect to be represented. Lifelong cops watching over cops can be a really bad idea. The creators of the qualifications required to become sheriff knew that, hence even the town trash man can hold the position. Ask yourself this. Where do you think the loyalties are of a person who has served in law enforcement their entire working career? With their buddies in blue or with the voters who elected them to a job for four years they can't even be fired from?

It was a small crowd, but interested. Since they weren't privy to enough information to know whether or not Kochanowski was telling the truth, it's hard to tell what effect it had on them. However, when I pointed out that I hadn't even met the guy until that very morning, over four years after my son's death, their ears seemed to prick up a bit. He had made various statements about how his office was open to all residents of the county. I pointed out that he was again lying and his statements must only true if I didn't live in Saline County.

I didn't win, but I didn't really expect to and it wasn't my primary goal. One thing that's important to know is if you want to win an election in Saline County, or Kansas really for that matter, don't run as a Democrat. I did garner around 26 percent of the vote, nearly six thousand voters. So basically, only 1 out of 4 of Saline County voters thought it was wrong for law enforcement officials to violate constitutional rights and help killers get away. If the fact that the voter turnout wasn't even fifty percent is taken into account, the real numbers are that less than 1 out of 8 county residents disapproved of the SO's behavior. Kind of sad, but at least it was a start.

I'd like to think running had its intended purpose, to make citizens aware. My campaign was a complete success if I prevented a single other family from going through the hell the authorities had drug us through. I told the newspaper as much when they called for my reaction after the election.

Chapter 26

Even though Judge Hellmer had essentially refused to let us conduct discovery in the malicious prosecution suit against Ray and Jessie, pending appeal, it made little difference to the case. Getting answers to the questions posed to them would be nice, but more so for the wrongful death lawsuit that was just getting under way. In fact, we moved for summary judgment in the malicious prosecution case based on the overwhelming evidence that already existed.

All of this had the desired effect on Ray. We were coming after him hard and heavy, his lawyer was costing a lot of money, and it was going to drag on for who knew how long. These were powerful tools for our side and gave us the leverage we needed to take it to the next level.

Meanwhile, having finally figured out what his future in Salina was going to be like if I had anything to do with it, Ray had decided to join the Air Force and get out of town. They wanted him in October of 2006. If he left town and missed court appearances and depositions, he would certainly lose both suits. He could probably live with a malicious prosecution conviction, though I suppose there could have been some ramifications to his budding military career, but a wrongful death conviction would lead to financial reparations. In other words, he would likely have to work his entire life with much of his pay going to us. Desperate to make it all go away, he and Jessie agreed to make a deal with us.

We proposed they take polygraph tests. If they passed, we would go away. If not, things would keep going the way they had been. They jumped at the opportunity. The only caveat was we would need to conduct pre-polygraph interviews with them in order to gain information for the polygraph examiner to use in formulating questions. Ray and Jessie agreed, but stipulated neither I nor Theresa could be present for the interviews. Though brazen liars, apparently doing it to our faces across the table was still a stretch for them. We agreed to their condition.

Though it's tempting to focus on the actual polygraph portion of the exercise, that wasn't where the value was for us. They would have to sit down, attorney beside them, and explain the sequence of events that night. We couldn't get too aggressive since they could get up and leave at any time, but nonetheless, they would have to answer questions. Jack Sheahon, their attorney, was just as much in the dark as anyone since they lied to him as much as they did to everybody else, so he didn't play much of a factor. Other than what was outright obvious, he wouldn't begin to know which questions or statements were even significant to us.

As a seasoned defender of lowlife, having Ray and Jessie plead the Fifth Amendment, even though he likely had no idea what the hell was really going on, was probably a smart move personally. Was it the smartest move legally? I doubt it, but a guy's got to watch out for his own neck. Ray and Jessie were the clients from hell. They didn't have any money, they lied incessantly to the only person willing to defend them, and Ray quite possibly did something very bad to a person that went to the same high school Jack's daughter was attending. In fact, his daughter was friends with Destry's youngest brother, Lucas.

One of the few satisfying moments in the whole debacle happened to involve Jack. Since I was still in charge of what little money Ray had left in his so called education fund, an awkward position if there ever was one, I gave Ray a check for around $9,000 on his twenty-first birthday. Not only was it Ray's money, I wanted to make sure Jack got paid at least something for his trouble, though I knew I couldn't necessarily make that happen.

What I could do though was make sure Jack knew they got the money. So at one of the meetings, we just happened to casually throw in that the Allens had finished all business with Ray by just recently giving him this money. Jack didn't look up, but he seemed to hesitate in his writing momentarily. Hopefully, he was able to squeeze some out of them for his efforts.

Ray and Jessie were told the questions were vital for the polygraph examiner to get the feel of the case and to know what to ask. There was a thread of truth in the statement, but from our perspective, the true value was getting them to sit down and talk again, something we were powerless to do before we had the lawsuits as leverage. Our only questioning up to this point was in the stalking hearing they brought against me over a year before.

This is an element I need to comment on. As a regular person, something I think I was until June of 2004, I never was confronted with the cold, hard truth about the system. The reality is this. If law enforcement doesn't want to do their job, there is nothing you can do to make them. Sure, it's a violation of your civil rights, but what are you going to do? Justice is a function of cash and there is usually an exponent involved. Only they have the ability to compel witnesses to speak, or have access to certain records and databases.

We, as I believe most Americans do, had complete faith in a system that went out of its way to not do its job. Talk about feeling abandoned. As a regular person, you can do nothing but what we did, something our attorney had never actually heard of anyone doing before. Pursue justice on your own dime and somehow get the court system involved, which Ray and Jessie had so obligingly done with the stalking suit. Then let the hounds lose. Just make sure to bring your wallet if you dare try.

This brings up another point. Theresa and I weren't rich people when this whole thing began. We had nice things, lived in a nice house and went nice places. We raised good kids and saved our money for old age. I think in the tapestry of America, we would be considered solidly middle class folks. At the point we made our offer to Ray and Jessie to consent to the polygraph examination, we were closing in on spending nearly $150,000. We couldn't afford to keep going much longer. It had to stop. What's it worth to catch someone who killed your kid? Ask yourself sometime and try to answer truthfully.

I was confident Ray could pass the examination. It had been over two years and he believed everything that came out of his mouth. He always had. I didn't think Jessie really knew anything anyway, so it didn't really matter how hers came out. We just wanted them to talk. The fact they didn't want Theresa or myself there promised juicy tidbits. They didn't disappoint.

Ray and Jessie were questioned together with Chris, Kathern, and Gerard present on our side. Ray, Jessie, and Jack were on the other side of the table. The conversation was recorded. It began with some clarification about whether they were still exerting their 5th Amendment privileges, which they affirmed. When Chris pointed out to them the ramifications in civil court of pleading the Fifth, they replied they only did it because Jack told them to and besides, they had already answered the questions and didn't want to do it again.

What Chris meant by ramifications is the fact that, unlike criminal proceedings, in civil court the jury can take into consideration the fact defendants invoke the fifth. Many jurors tend to think one has something to hide when they invoke the fifth. In other words, in both our malicious prosecution lawsuit and wrongful death lawsuit, the juries would be able to take into consideration they, Ray and Jessie, were hiding something and feared conviction if whatever it was came out. Obviously, that wouldn't have been a good thing for their defense. Had our true desire been simply to win the lawsuits, we never would have had them submit to polygraph examinations. We had enough it was a done deal. We didn't need them to win.

Then it began. Jessie started with attacking us, stating we were like two-year-old children, always asking the same questions. What she was talking about was anyone's guess. The only time she had even spoken with us was in court during the stalking hearing, and none of the questions we were asking had come up then.

One thing she conveniently didn't mention was the fact she perjured herself in regards to the time they were with Tommy, so technically, she had answered that question before, just not with the same answer. We really just stayed away from the whole topic, other than what she was willing to volunteer without asking. Questioning her about why she committed perjury regarding to her alibi at the time of a homicide would only incense her and possibly send her packing. While amusing, that wasn't particularly productive. The fact she committed perjury was enough for us.

Regarding Tommy, they now both asserted he left before Destry even drove by, meaning he had left the scene near midnight or before, an hour and a half before he called to let Ray and Jessie know he had arrived home safely. Jessie, who was so concerned about Tommy's safety that she requested he call her when he got home, wasn't so concerned that she bothered to call him in that hour and a half time frame. Since Tommy stated in his deposition he only had a few beers and went directly home, he wouldn't have even been drunk when he called her, if he ever was, yet he supposedly couldn't even remember the call at all.

It was in this meeting Jessie made her assertions about my fixation with her breasts. She was simply beaming when she recounted the story. Other than attacking us, she really didn't have anything substantive to add. When talking with Ray, the investigative team again treaded lightly, but some questions were so obvious they had to be asked. Why didn't Ray mention the phone call he made to Destry that night?

Though he had spoken previously of how he did tell me about the phone call, he had allowed it wasn't until a week later. That was a lie, but not relevant to the opening he had left. He was asked why he didn't bring it up the day Destry was found dead. He responded it just didn't seem important. When it was pointed out to him he took the time to recount to us how Destry had driven by him that night, waving and smiling, he said he did that just to make us feel better.

Ray: Because it's a grim situation, I wanted people to feel the best. I don't know. Destry was happy, he was always happy. To me he was a great person so. And plus, I also believe it was an accident, so.

Again, Ray was asked why he didn't tell about the phone call later. He said he just didn't see how that would help anything. Besides, there were more important things to worry about.

Ray: I, I don't know. I mean I remember that I brought it up because we were, he was asking if I'd hung out with him. I may have mentioned it before, it may have slipped my mind but, I mean it wasn't like number one on my priority list to say hey, I talked to Destry that night, just so you'll know. I mean, the more important thing at hand was that Destry was dead and nobody knew why. I mean, talking to Destry for four minutes about goin' to sleep and to the festival wasn't a priority in my life. I didn't see that as being important. I don't know, I admit I overlooked it but...

Chris: I'm just trying to understand why you didn't think that was important.

Ray: Because there was a larger factor at stake. Destry was dead and nobody knew why. He was a deacon at the church, he had good grades. Talking about whether or not he was going to bed and studying for the festival didn't seem like an important detail, I don't know. It just didn't seem important.

The most significant detail to come from the meeting was one thrown in by Ray, seemingly intended to be an off the cuff remark since nobody asked him. Kathern was asking Ray details about the morning Destry was found. Ray had been maintaining he woke up and drove right to the restaurant where Jessie worked.

Kath: Um, so you went to the restaurant to see Jess. Can you go through the morning?

Ray: I went there to get breakfast and, uh, I thought it was odd on the way there on Marymount I saw Bart driving Destry's car, but, uh, I mean it was a new car. Destry, you know, maybe got in trouble, got it taken away, I don't know. And Jess and I were talkin' and I was going over after that to talk with Bart.

Why in the world would he throw in this seemingly insignificant detail out of the blue? It had nothing to do with the question. I believe the reason was because he read on the website we created in Destry's memory that in court he testified to knowing about the death nearly an hour before I called 911 and three full hours before our pastor actually informed him. Ray felt compelled to offer an explanation, even though nobody asked. Though he never tied it together for us, undoubtedly, if actually asked about the discrepancy, he would answer he was referring to seeing me at that time and his mind did the reverse math without him knowing about it. So, when he was asked about the time he found out about Destry in court, he was really referring to what time he saw me drive by because after thinking about it over all that must have been when I found Destry.

There were a couple of important problems with his spontaneous revelation. Number one, I didn't drive home the way he was referring to. Additionally, I hadn't told anybody I drove Destry's car home from the Depot rather than the pickup I went out in, yet Ray knew. Having temporarily lost my mind, I couldn't find the key to the pickup I had driven out in, so I took Destry's car when I returned home.

Ray's contention I would just drive by him without noticing him was absurd. I bought the damn truck Ray was driving around in. I would certainly remember seeing him. And lastly, before 9 a.m., I drove by the place he stated he was sleeping, twice in fact, and his truck wasn't there. The location was only a couple of hundred yards down the street from where we lived. It would have been impossible to not notice it.

160

Yet, Ray did know I was driving the car between 9:45 and 10 a.m., even though he had left the neighborhood nearly an hour before. How? I believe it was because he was waiting in the anonymous parking lot of an extensive apartment complex that was located on the way to the Depot, waiting for the show to begin. He certainly would've recognized Destry's car coming by.

There was another problem with his timeline. According to him, after he woke up, he headed, out of his way I might add, for the restaurant where Jessie worked. This indirect route happened to take him down the same street I was supposedly returning home on in Destry's car. Then he proceeded directly to the restaurant and ate. He was certain of these details. The only problem was that the restaurant didn't open for another hour, at 11 a.m., yet he made no mention of waiting around. He and Jessie seemed to have forgotten to go over some of the details of their story.

Additionally, around 10:15 that morning, he was seen by Nichole driving through the park where the Smoky Hill River Festival was to take place. After speaking with me, she went out searching for Destry for herself and since he was supposed to be working over in the park, she went by there. Obviously, she didn't find Destry, but she did find Ray. The park wasn't even close to being on the way to the restaurant. Why would he omit this detail and, more importantly, why was he in the vicinity of where Destry was expected to be?

When asked about the conversation with his Aunt Theresa regarding the alcohol, methamphetamine, and expressing regret for some vague action, he stated it simply never took place. In other words, Theresa made it up completely and I made up witnessing it. Ray was never as clever as he thought he was and this proclamation is a good example. Why not just say sure, he'd had a conversation with her but he was talking about Adam? Say we must have simply misunderstood him? It made a hell of a lot more sense than completely denying the existence of a conversation with three witnesses, especially when it's common knowledge that if any one of the three was an established liar, it was him.

The last tidbit was nearly as good as my supposed breast fixation. As he had theorized with Sandy, I was growing a lot of weed out at the Depot. That was one of the reasons he and Destry had visited three weeks before his death, near the middle of May, to see the pot growing. When they arrived though, there wasn't anything, just a bunch of empty coffee cans where the plants had supposedly been. Ray was asked if he went up to the loft, where he stated the pot was growing, he said he started to go up a couple of steps, but then stopped and retreated back down.

Why would a person go up two steps and turn around? What happened in the time that elapsed in those two steps to cause you to change your mind? It was a strange response and another odd detail that could just as easily have been avoided altogether if he had just said he didn't go up at all. I suspect he was trying to split the difference between not going up and telling me he had.

When he had been at our house on September 8 of 2004, during my questioning I brought up several topics he must have taken to heart when he had time to think about them later. For instance, when he told me Jessie was with him that night, so she would be an alibi, I responded by opining I didn't think her word would be worth much since she was his girlfriend. This resulted in Tommy's name being brought into the fray.

I had also asked him about the Depot and his visit with Destry and, after hem hawing around so my intended question wouldn't seem obvious, I asked him if he had been up on the loft and looked down at the great view. He affirmed he had. This is notable because if a person does what I asked Ray about, the gun, sitting on top of the kitchen cabinet below, would be very obvious. Now when asked, he hadn't gone up there at all. He seemed to have recognized the significance of the detail.

The ashtray full of bullets, though not brought up in this meeting, was another point of fixation for Ray. When I brought up the topic of spent casings being found at the scene at our meeting on September 8, I purposefully didn't mention the ashtray at all. Ray also wanted to know more from Sandy about the ashtray and where it was, which she didn't know. Related or not, the one fact of the matter is the empty casings shouldn't have been in with the live ammo.

That was one of the family rules when we were target shooting. Putting the spent casings back in with the live is akin to putting the empty peanut shells back in with the peanuts when you're eating them. It makes it increasingly difficult to pick the live from the spent. So, what person didn't know the rules when shooting, since Destry always did?

Additionally, though Destry would have been allowed to target shoot if desired, it wasn't a subject that really needed to come up if he could avoid it. Not that there was anything wrong with it, but I would undoubtedly ask other questions. I always did. Destry consistently left the place immaculate, according to Nichole, because he didn't want anything to be out of place and cause questions to be asked. Leaving empty casings in with the live rounds simply wouldn't have been acceptable to him.

We've always been curious why it was on the table at all. The gun was already loaded and Destry knew it. Why bring bullets over to the table when they were stored in an entirely separate location from the gun? Possibly someone else didn't realize we kept the gun loaded. Whatever the case, it was a topic that held a lot of interest for Ray.

As the meeting drew to a close, we requested DNA from both of them. We told them we had found condoms at the scene and were trying to find out who had used them. We knew Ray probably hadn't but given his manly attitude and his desire to clear himself of having sex with someone other than Jessie, since she was standing there when we asked, he was eager to give the sample. What I mean by manly attitude is that he would never wear a condom. That wasn't how real men rolled, so sure, he would give a sample, since they couldn't possibly be his. Jessie also gave a sample. It apparently never occurred to them, or their lawyer, there are other uses for DNA.

Chapter 27

With the preliminary meeting out of the way, Ray and Jessie were set to take the polygraph exams a few days later. It wasn't as easy as just showing up, taking the test, and leaving. There would be another information gathering session with the examiner, Gary, an ex-law enforcement professional. Jessie went first.

She was asked what she thought she was there for. When reading the transcript, I found myself often wondering if she was even talking about the same thing we were. Jessie rambles on and on, Gary asking questions intermittently. After cutting through all the guff, the basic gist of her story was she believed Destry killed himself, though she admitted having no idea why he would want to do that. She and Ray had been brainstorming and they thought the reason we were after them was because we believed Ray talked Destry into killing himself during the phone call, thus we believed Ray was responsible for his death. If anything, she postulated Destry committed suicide because he had such a tough childhood.

Jessie: I truly think he [Destry] had a rough childhood, ya'
know. Bart is a rough guy, he is and, he's kind a
creepy too. That's a girl's stand point, ya' know. Ya'
know, the old man wandering eye is creepy from any
young child, ya' know, girl, and he has it, ya' know.
And Theresa's just, I know Theresa from way back, I
mean before all this. My dad was good friends with
her dad. We are years apart, her children are more
my age, ya' know, than I'm her age, but she has got a
long history of drug abuse, alcohol abuse. She lost an
older sister to alcohol and drunk driving, stuff like
that. And she always, when I seen her, she always
seemed wired.

As I have said, Jessie's an expert on everything, even things
she knows nothing about. Her source of information is Ray, her
own fertile imagination, and her self-professed terrible life,
which she goes on and on about. She pities Ray for believing in
family in any way, because she knows it's a bunch of crap. Gary
never once asks her about her life or background, but she spends
the better part of five minutes bitching about how hard her
childhood was, how much she dislikes her stepmother and vice
versa, and how her dad is gutless. For the record, Jessie didn't
know Theresa from way back and her father, the general, wasn't
friends in any way, much less good friends, with Theresa's
father. Jessie's father wouldn't even attend her marriage to Ray.

Jessie informs Gary she knows all about polygraphs because
she did a debate on them when she was a freshman in high
school. For instance, she knew that polygraph examinations
weren't "dismissable" in court. She also declared herself an
expert on suicides.

Jessie: I've seen a lot of death, in time, ya' know. I'm only 21
and I've gone through a lot for 21 and I've seen a lot of
death and I've seen a lot of suicide, ya' know, a lot of
it, ya' know. A lot of my family members have
committed suicide, a lot of, um, my friends have, ya'
know, and he was such a quiet guy and he didn't ever

talk to us about what he was about. What's up? Nothin'. Ya' know, he never talked. He was always interested in what was wrong with us. What was goin' on with us, never the opposite way.

She said a mouthful there. Destry was always interested in them and their troubles, but they couldn't care less about his. I doubt she realized how bad it sounded, but I appreciated her candor. Jessie talks about how she was such a good girl and how she never had sex before eighteen. She never drank, nor did drugs. She felt it simply wasn't right and since she had such a strong moral compass, trashed anyone who believed differently. Jessie was the bulldog saint.

When Gary asks her what we thought she did she replies,

Jessie: They think me, me, nothing. They just can go after you, 'cause they can. That's what I've been told. And I think that's a little wrong, but if they want to, they are. I think it's because they can't get to Ray. I am the door and they can't get to him. Ya' know, if it was just Ray by himself, I think they could have got him pretty good, ya' know. I reamed him [Ray] pretty good but I'm in his life, ya' know, so, they can't just go after him without goin' after me. There'd be no point.

So, Jessie was the door to Ray and without her, he would have gotten caught. One other interesting comment she makes, and emphasizes, is that when Ray came to her restaurant to inform her of Destry's death, he didn't know how Destry had died. She expressly stated all he knew was that he had passed away during the night.

At one point, she brings up the stalking hearing, the questioning she and Ray were subjected to, and how she always told the truth.

Jessie: If we got caught for perjury, which I am not doin', I hope, I am not doin' it 'cause I think that's stupid. Just tell the truth. Perjury, you get more life time jail than a premeditated murder, I think.

Gary tolerates most of her nonsensical ramblings well enough, at least until the examination was over, at which point she exclaims that it was fun. Gary tells her she either "needs to get a life, or is a liar", sort of a satirical statement from a guy whose job is to detect lies.

All in all, we felt it was a success, at least as much as could be expected. Jessie revealed, whether she meant to or not, how much her family life had scarred her and influenced her beliefs and thoughts. She also revealed several pieces of hard information, one in particular, which was very useful to our case. The restaurant where she worked didn't open until 11 a.m. and Ray didn't come before that time the morning Destry was found. Ray's opportunity to talk was the afternoon of the same day.

The rules were explained to Ray as they were to Jessie. Gary asked him to tell him why he was there, to start at the beginning. I'll let Ray's own words, as transcribed, tell his story.

Ray: At the beginning Destry committed suicide, and through the course of our relationship we were never that close, as friends, except when we were very young children. Um, so after, like, I was in an accident on March 6, 2004, which is when my best friend died. It's still hard to talk about, but, um, so after you know, my best friend passed away. I was lost, I was confused. I didn't sleep very well. My mom kicked me out and I didn't understand why. You know, I wanted to have that comfort and I didn't know why. Um, I really looked for someone to talk to and it happened to be Destry. So without making this a soap opera, um, you know, I guess I can understand why the behavior was odd. All of a sudden we're hangin' out all the time, and spending time together. Uh, I guess one night he and his girlfriend got into a fight, an argument I understand, um, and he committed suicide. And since then that odd behavior that I displayed, though odd at that time before. After my friend passed away, and before Destry passed away, and given my past of being a liar and a cheat, my way or the highway option. Um, they found that with the phone call made to him before he died and us seeing him, they felt that we might know more than we are leading on, but we don't. So that's really what we're doin' here today.

The examiner asked him once again to start at the beginning.

Ray: Um, well after, before my best friend passed away um, I was in a, I got charged with DWI in Arkansas and I've never had a speeding ticket, um, you know. We come from a very respectable family, you know, you have to remember my family, at least, anyway.

My Aunt Jennifer is a doctor, my grandpa is a very prominent business man, my Uncle Bart is the same, and my Aunt Theresa was a really good mom, took care of the kids, stayed home, didn't have a job. She raised the kids. You know, we come from a family of, you know, respect. And I kind a used that to my advantage in my life, I took that name, I took that life style, and ah, then I flew with it. Okay, and in that way, I hurt a lot of people, said a lot of things that were hurtful and mean, and I cheated and lied. I built this horrible reputation for myself and I just didn't care and, uh, when I got that DWI it was a wake-up call and I came back to Salina and started reevaluating things, very slowly. It wasn't like I had an epiphany.

And, uh, started trying to reassess what I wanted to do with my life, then me and my friend get in this accident, and really from that day is when it happened. My eyes woke up that my careless actions, and living life the way I was at full throttle, without ever checking left or right, had its consequences. And, um, that's really when I started thinkin' this, this is not the way to live. Being more honest and more open and, and you know it was hard. It still is. The first thing I wanted to do, the first, first time I wanted to be honest. I wanted to be honest and not lie was to Adam's life. She needed to know the truth.

And then I got into this cloud. I couldn't sleep. I had a hard time remembering things. Um, they thought it was from the pneumonia, ah, not pneumonia but, oh, dang it, I'm at a loss for words. Hypothermia. Then I started hangin' out with my cousin Destry, and I really had no apparent goals. All I knew at that point was, in that cloud that I was living in, of life being so real, was that I needed to get on my feet. I needed to do what was right, and you know I look back at my past and I realize the kind of person I was and, um, I really confided in Destry a lot cause we had that history. When we were kids we shared a lot. We hung out, I mean at night after the midnight hours, we hung out at the cross, next to the river, right down the road from where he lived so it was easy for him to sneak out and hang out with us. Um, we just, we just had so much to catch up on 'cause we spent probably six or seven years apart, and we had such a close tie when we were younger. And then one night he drove by and, uh, he was with his girlfriend, and I guess they had been on the rocks a little bit, and, uh, he made a habit every time we went out, or every time he went home he'd come down and hang out with us and he didn't come back by that night. So we called and said what's goin' on and he [Destry] said ah, I'm tired I got the festival, the river festival this month, was starting up the next morning, the next day, here in Salina. And ah, he said "No, I'm tired I don't want to go out, I'm in a band tomorrow, we're going to play, and I'm tired," said we didn't see you drive by, what happened? He said "Oh, I took the back way home," which, I guess, without getting to technical but it's just a longer way around the city, country roads back to his house, cause that curve, you can't see anything from the middle of the street 'cause it has a big arc and his driveway you can't see from over there. So okay, fine, and I still tried convincin' him, like come on man and you know the kind of stuff. Come on, you been out till four in the morning before, come on, but he didn't want to come out so I said, well alright. I'll see you at the festival tomorrow, I don't know what I said but it was to the effect of I'll see you tomorrow

And, uh, I was living in my truck at the time and, uh, at the cross and I got up that morning, the following morning and got in my truck and went to my fiancé, my fiancé, my girlfriend's work. And I saw Bart driving the Mercedes on Marymount, which I can understand. Destry was kind of a carefree, rebellious type so, I thought maybe he got his car taken away, or something, and I went down to the restaurant. I didn't have any money, no way to live. I was in that delusional state of trying to find a way to live. Um, I went there to get my food, and she [Jessie] bought food for me. I proceeded to go to my Uncle Bart's house just to talk to him, you know, he was kind of helping me get on my feet. He paid for my lawyer fees for the, uh, backpack they found with some paraphernalia in it.

He just really tried to help me. He wanted to be a family member, he wanted to help and, uh, when I showed up there was a lot of cars, and the pastor was there and I thought that was kind of odd, but everybody was looking for Destry at that point. So I guess Nichole, his girlfriend, had called my girlfriend lookin' for him.

The pastor walked up and said Destry's dead. Man, I dropped my phone, I dropped everything, and fell to the ground. Um, went and told Jessie about what had happened, um, and then, like a week after that, Bart took me to the Depot. And after hearing that Destry died I went back in to that cloud, I lost track of everything. I didn't know what time it was, I couldn't tell you anything, what day it was then. Um, and he took me out to the Depot and I can't remember what was said, but he said to a point, that he thought I had somethin' to do with it. And he finally grabbed my hands and he kept telling me if, the fact of, if you were here, if you were hanging out with him, if you know something, tell us if you know something. I just finally shouted "I DIDN'T KILL YOUR SON!" and then I ran out. There's no lights in this area and it's really dark. He chased me down, ran up to me and hugged me like a linebacker would. He just plowed into me and hugged me and said I love you, I'll always love you, I'm your uncle and everything, you had nothin' to do with this' and I kind a let it go 'cause, 'cause Bart's been very cold to me my whole life and he's just kind of a, he's just very stone cold. He's just very forward, the kind who'll tell you what he thinks. I wish he didn't but, whatever. And after that I spent time at their house, I helped mow the lawn.

And then one day I was at work and Destry's girlfriend come up to me and said, well, the Allen's have been investigating Destry's death and they think you might have something to do with it. And it blew me away that my family, this is family that I spent every holiday with. Christmas, birthdays, Easter, slumber parties, weekends, everything, to where, you know, it blew me away that they would think that. I understand that my past, I cheated a lot, I stole, I didn't have a name that said dependable next to it and, uh, I just went over and confronted them about it and Bart danced around the issue a little bit but finally Theresa came in and said "Yes, we do" and that's when it immediately sunk in that they thought I was seriously involved. No questions asked, they would die, by their death, be saying they believe I was the one that took their son's life. To this day even. I'm getting more past it but still it's unbelievable, I couldn't believe I heard it.

And, uh, pretty much we lived in a house at 111 Delaware shortly after and we were getting letters on our car that said pack your bags, get your soap ready, how can you live with yourself with Destry's picture on it. People callin' us. I got tailed through town. Friends I've known asked me "Did you really do it?" We lived in an area where Bart would drive by going to work and there would be days we counted he went by at least a dozen times. And we felt so cornered and so pressured that we didn't know what to do.

We just finally went, a policeman saw them going by [when we were talking to her] and said you should go get a PFA, it will help. And we did. We went and filed it and, uh, we just wanted to have some safety, we wanted to feel like we weren't being cornered, preyed on, and, uh, we had a hearing and their lawyer was a bulldog, needless to say.

We, uh, didn't have an attorney, didn't know we needed one. We're 19, we're still kids at that time. We still are. What do you want? He asked every question. Did you do it? Were you there? Did you hold the gun? Um, and then, uh, that was the malicious case and now looking back on it, yeah we were, not knowing the law. As not frightened, but in a state of constant alert, we needed some closure and it seemed like the best answer without being narrow minded, and being irrational. It seemed like a legal, legitimate way to get them to back off. We understand, we got the notes from you, but just please back off.

Now we're dealin' with the wrongful death which is linked to the phone call that we made to him. I know I'm leavin' a lot of stuff out but really since my best friend passed away I've just had this hard time dealin' with this. My wife's own family didn't come to our wedding because we got some wind that my family

was goin' to show up with assault rifles. Um, I've
had friends drive from Montana and KC and ask
did you really do it. I thought you committed suicide.

It's just the world that I'm surrounded in is real,   and it's
more real than I've ever experienced, and it's, you know, I
guess, now I've kind a turned my faith a little bit. Like I
said, that when my friend died, there's been just too many
anomalies, signs that maybe there is a God up there, but I
don't know. I've turned my faith a little bit. You know
there's always that eternal question from Darwin of why,
ya know, why this, why that. And I just don't understand
how after spending so many years with a family, with so
many close ties that, yeah, they can resent me, yes, they can
say "No, you can't stay the night," or "No, you can't drive
our car." But pretty much that's where we are today. And
we just want to put a stop to it.

Gary: How did this whole scenario start that they thought
         you were involved in this to start with. How did that
         happen?

Ray: There was this phone call that was made to Destry.

Gary: How did they know that?

Ray: They acquired his phone records. After he passed   away
         the forensic team that went in and evaluated, you   know,
         the blood pattern, the body position, the gun   position.
         They showed 'em all this stuff and they   started   going
         through his phone and found the recent   calls   made   to
         Destry and my wife's phone number was one of those, my
         girlfriend at the time. Her phone number was one of the
         numbers that was entered in the phone and it had a time
         next to it from when it was called, and, well, there was an
         estimated time of death that put our phone call, I mean it
         was right before the time of death and they felt that
         somehow in that four minutes that we had spoken, that,
         uh, I had convinced him or had told him something to the
         affect of your life's not worth anything, you know, you
         need to die. Die, disappear, nothing. You leave this world.
         And they thought that my presence, with Destry, uh, at the
         time we were hanging out compared to months before,

years before we weren't. They just felt that my behavior was odd, that, you know, we had spent so much time together, in that little amount of time. When you spend so much time together when it's opposed to, between 1997 and 2003, we really didn't see each other except for holidays. So they felt that because of the odd behavior I was demonstrating, the phone call being made so close to the time of death, uh, they felt it reasonable that there was, that I was, that I would be the one to suspect if anything.

"Your life's not worth anything, you know, you need to die. Die, disappear, nothing. You leave this world." Pretty strong words, if you ask me. At another point, Gary asks Ray about the conversation he had with his Aunt Theresa about taking methamphetamine and doing something he regretted.

Ray: My Aunt Theresa says that somewhere in this deal we had a discussion and I made some reference to using methamphetamine, or what do they call it, speed, or somethin'. I told her I was doin' that and made some horrible mistake. I honestly can't recall ever having that conversation. I know, I had conversations with her, I did. Some of the conversations were one on one, um, but no, I couldn't recall that conversation. I couldn't even give you a single word said in the conversation.

Gary: Were you doing crank at the time, anytime?

Ray: No.

Gary: Why would she say you were doing that if you didn't, who gives a shit if you're doing crank. It's water under the bridge, who cares? This is important. Why would she say you told her that? You need to keep in mind I can't tell the difference between a little or a big lie. They're all the same. This is your chance to make this go away. Don't try and cast things in a light most favorable to you. Just lay your cards on the table and it will be okay.

Ray: That's what I'm telling you, I honestly to God, I can't remember it, it might have been, if my, if my memory was a video tape there would be a lot of scrambled images, there would be a lot of static.

Gary: It's not.

Ray: I'm just sayin' if it were…

Gary: But it's not, it's not for any of us.

Ray: Well, like I said when my best friend passed away, I had the whole world right here, nobody could bother me. Nobody could touch me and after my best friend passed away, it crumbled, it was too real. I'd never…You see that kind a stuff on Maximum Exposure. Oh no, that'll never happen to me. I'll never get cancer, or I'll never get an STD. You always say that to yourself. I hear people say that all the time. When I got my DWI, I never thought I'd get that and I did. And just to be put in the place of being accused of not only being involved in the accident that I was in, but with my cousin, I don't know. Like I said my world's changed 180, 360 degrees in those three months and for me remembering those…I personally feel I block a lot of it out intentionally, because I don't want to remember it. It's too real. I can't even see my siblings before I leave for the military. I haven't seen 'em for six months. I had a weekly visit with 'em. I'd take 'em to school, take 'em to breakfast but because of the situation I'm in now I have no contact with my brothers and that hurts because now they've heard the story and now they're going to grow up thinking, "Did he really do it?" I don't care what other people think, they can think whatever they want, but my brothers, it's just too personal. He [Bart] sent a letter to their dad about this. I can look at you right now and tell you I do not remember ninety percent of anything that happened in the last two years involving this.

They continue with the conversation. At this point, they've been talking for nearly an hour. Ray is testing Gary's patience. The topic of Ray's character comes up.

Gary: And then, apparently your credibility is not too good?

Ray: No, it's not very good.

Gary: Well, let's try and just shore that up just a tad.

Ray: Okay.

Gary: I'm not trying to make it perfect but we can shore it up a little.

Ray: Alright.

Gary: Here's what I'm thinking, but if you have a problem with it, you'll need to tell me, alright? Prior to Destry's death do you remember blaming someone else for something you did? Because that's what they think you did.

Ray: That's kind of an open ended question.

Gary: No, it's not.

Ray: Well that could be to any scenario. That could be Adam, that could be Destry, that could be my mom…

Gary: I don't have a clue, don't know you very well. Do you make a habit of that, with not taking responsibility for your actions?

Ray: Well, I used to not do that, but like I said I'm trying to take responsibility now, so, read it over. My mind is going 180 miles an hour.

Gary: Prior to Destry's death do you remember blaming someone else for something you did?
          Do you have a problem with that?

Ray: Not immediately, no. Well no, I, I understand what you're sayin' but, I mean, I'm not educated, so…

Gary: Don't give me that crap, your fairly articulate. Don't blow smoke up my skirt.

Ray: Huh?

Gary: Don't blow smoke up my skirt.

Ray: That question seems to me, it's almost like…

Gary: People don't think much of you do they?

Ray: No, they don't.

Gary: I'm trying to get you some questions that will give you character.

Ray: Okay.

Gary:	Unless you don't have any.
Ray:	I'd like to think that I have character. That's not a good thing to ask.
Gary:	The world's not full of perfect folks.
Ray:	Okay.
Gary:	Trying to give you character, trying to show that there is redeeming social value in your background and that when it gets to the nut cutting, you have both oars in the water.
Ray:	Okay.

Ray is given the examination and they were done. The conversation was one of the most lucid I had ever heard Ray participate in, even including the lies he throws in. If my attempt were to paint him a failure of the education system and a lunatic, I would enclose even more of the conversation.

Unlike Jessie, I'm not an expert on polygraphs. The way Gary administered the examinations, they were allowed to pick the questions they wanted to answer. They were informed that if any of the questions made them uncomfortable, the examiner would change them. At one point, Ray asks what would happen if he ran for it. Gary's response was his job would be easier if that happened, he couldn't care less what Ray did. Ray seemed surprised and relieved. In general, it was a pretty stress free experience for both of them.

As mentioned, we just wanted them to sit and talk and from that perspective, it was a total success. Though television fails to mention this nuance it's the only real value in polygraph examinations. By themselves, they are literally worthless, but as part of a multifaceted investigatory arsenal, they can be quite useful. As I expected and hoped, they both passed the test.

Jessie was never really a target and we never suspected she knew anything anyway. Ray, who told the examiner several documented lies while conversing, believes everything he says. Believing what you say is helpful for passing polygraph tests.

Everything was over. Ray left the next week for basic training to go into the USAF. He successfully graduated and he, with Jessie in tow, left to defend the United States of America. God help us all.

What Happened?

What happened at the Depot in the early morning hours of June 10, 2004? Unfortunately, it's likely no one will ever know for sure. If Destry was killed, as we allege, by his cousin Ray Jones and if he ever admitted it, could his version of events ever be believed, given his lifelong record of deceit and evasion of responsibility? Not likely. His story would always be slanted to cast himself in the best light. As such, we feel obligated to put forth our version of events for those who, like ourselves, are asking themselves, what happened to Destry Allen?

Destry had a really good day on Wednesday, June 9. He always looked forward to working at the Smoky Hill River Festival. There are only a couple of days allotted to setting up all the tents and other equipment and it can only be accomplished because the workers are, for the most part, the same cast of characters from one year to the next. Destry really liked becoming one of the few who actually knew the ins and outs of the set-up and the respect that came with the knowledge. He was getting to know everyone and it was really neat to be part of such an impressive and appreciated community project.

We had suggested he attend a week long mechanical engineering course the week before up at Kansas State University, which he did gladly but not without some protestation as it did cut in to the first week of his summer. Nevertheless he managed to have a good time learning and returned from KSU on Friday, June 4, so his summer didn't really begin until that Monday, June 7. He worked at his summer job on Monday and Tuesday. While at the festival on Wednesday, June 9, he undoubtedly saw and spoke with Ray, who was also helping out somehow or another and was only there because of Destry. At Ray's insistence, he made arrangements to meet him at the Depot after he was done spending time with Nichole. Before his week at KSU, he had been spending some late nights at Adam's Cross with Ray, so getting together late at night was par for the course and the Depot was a mere three miles away. The only difference would be they wouldn't be sitting on the ground with cars driving by.

In the evening, Destry met up with Nichole at our house and they spent time resolving some important aspects of their relationship, according to Nichole. Theresa and I were just going to bed when they left, the assumption on our part that he was following her home and would be back pretty soon, like usual. We both agreed it had been a big day for him with a bigger one tomorrow, since it was the day before the festival with work yet to be done. Additionally, one of his good friends was actually playing in a band at the pre-festival concert that Thursday evening. He had his new/used Mercedes we bought for him and with it came the knowledge that we were happy with and supportive of his growth as a young man. Life was good. I heard the door shut and fell asleep.

Destry followed Nichole south towards Adam's Cross, where they evidently saw Ray, according to Ray himself. When they arrived at the stop sign at Crawford Street, they parted company. Destry turned east toward the Depot and Nichole west to her brother's house, where she was to spend the night. Nichole assumed he was going to the Depot to meet Ray, who she knew Destry had been seeing but didn't like. Destry had cleaned up and put on fresh clothes, so she knew he was doing something, most likely with Ray. She even said as much in her interview with the SO more than once.

Nichole called Destry at 12:37 a.m. and they spoke for several minutes. This was the phone call the SO represented to me as the last Destry made. Destry told Nichole he loved her and would see her tomorrow. He continued to wait. At 1:07 a.m., he finally received a phone call from Ray on Jessie's phone. They spoke for over four minutes. Jessie had said in an interview Destry always was late and made them wait, so possibly they did the same to him, or having seen Destry and Nichole driving the same direction, assumed he would be busy with her for a while.

Ray told Destry he was sorry about the delay and would be right out. Ray had already drank a significant amount of Jack Daniel's and taken some methamphetamine leftover from his ill-fated trip down the river three months before. Destry was likely beginning to wind down, tired from the long day. Maybe Ray wanted to use the Depot for his party or maybe he was tired of sleeping in his truck night after night. More likely, Destry pressed him for the twenty dollars Ray owed him. Cash was a sore topic to Ray. Destry was fully aware of how much money I was giving to him. Ray, who had been nurturing a blossoming rage control complex, snapped.

How dare Destry ask for money! He had plenty - a newish car, a private getaway in the woods, a beautiful, sweet girlfriend, a bright future, loving parents, and unconditional support. Everything Ray never had and never would have. Ray went dark and suffered a psychotic break. He knew where the gun was because Destry had shown it to him when they had come out to the Depot several weeks earlier. They had even shot it. He let the hate and resentment flow unabated. When mixed with a long standing, untreated, sociopathic condition, alcohol and methamphetamines, it became a raging, uncontrollable inferno.

Destry didn't have a chance to react. Sitting when hit with the .22 long rifle slug, he slumped forward before he dropped to the floor, his class ring in his left hand. I'm sure the sobering, icy hand of reality slapped Ray pretty quickly, but not before he burst out through the screen door, literally breaking it down the middle and tearing the fabric. Damn Destry for forcing him to do it!

Unlike all the other times in his life, there was nowhere to run and hide and no one to blame. After all, Tommy and Jessie knew he left to go out to the Depot. Right about then, at 1:30 a.m., Tommy, or more likely Jessie, called Ray using Tommy's phone. Ray had taken Jessie's phone so he could let them know if they could move the party out there. Ray told them Destry wasn't interested and he was coming back to the cross.

He knew what he had to do. Maybe people would believe it was an accident, maybe they wouldn't, but the fact of the matter was that after his involvement in Adam's death three months earlier, this time it wasn't likely to go well. Even he realized that people would be unlikely to believe another hard luck story where another kid ends up dead with Ray standing by in the curtains. If nothing else, he would be screwed with the family and whatever money he mistakenly believed was there for him.

Making it look like Destry killed himself was the only option. Besides, what was done was done. His admitting responsibility wouldn't bring Destry back, so why take the blame or pay unnecessary penalties. Like usual, all that really mattered was saving himself.

The question for anyone in Ray's position at that point would be the same. What does a suicide look like? Ray thought he knew, after all, he had watched television, the source of nearly all of his learned responses in life. At that point, had he simply wiped his prints and thrown the gun on the floor, he would have probably gotten it pretty close, but that's not how they do it on television. Destry needed to be seated at the table, looking at the photo he happened to have with him, when he shot himself. That sounded right.

Ray moved the table and pushed Destry's body sideways back under the table, leaving his body positioned on his stomach, his left hand with the class ring and arm under his body, which was aligned in a perfectly straight manner. He placed the table and chairs back where they were. Destry vomited in response to the movement of his body, a typical reaction to severe brain trauma. Plus, he was beginning to bleed a lot, but predominantly out of his mouth and nose, not so much from the small hole in his forehead. This gave Ray the opportunity to press the gun to wound on Destry's head leaving the soot ring, hoping to simulate a contact wound, and attempted to wrap Destry's hand around the gun so fingerprints would indicate the gun had been in his hand.

The only thing left was to create the table scene. He placed the photo and the bloody gun the way he thought they should look, the way they always look on those television shows. The one big problem was he was forced to stand at the end of the table when creating his art, thus the photo is facing the end of the table and is over the blood trail, unless Destry wanted to look at a photo sideways before he shot himself. Additionally, likely without knowing it, Ray inadvertently got blood on his hand, which he unconsciously shook, leaving cast off blood droplets on the chair he was standing over.

After Ray pushed Destry's body into what he considered the proper position, he realized the vomit and other bodily fluids where Destry originally fell were in the wrong place. At that point, Ray took Destry's right arm, extended it and swept it back and forth in a breaststroke style movement, originating at his face and sweeping downward. He did this several times. Ray was hoping the movement would obscure the original location of the fluids. The table and chairs had already been put back in place and spatter struck the bottom of the chair and table, marking them for identification at a later date.

There was nothing to do about the broken screen door, but he did pull the main door shut behind him as he left his cousin drowning in his own blood and pulmonary edema foam, classical music playing in the background on the radio. Presumably, or hopefully rather, he would die pretty soon. What if he survived to tell the tale? That wouldn't be good.

When Ray returned to the cross, Tommy had likely already left, since the party was dead. Ray had to come up with something since Destry would be found sooner or later. He already had it figured out before he left the Depot, old hand at creative deception he was. After all, Jessie would believe anything Ray said. That was her one defining characteristic. Ray told Jessie he was worried about poor Des. He was awful bummed out when Ray left him at the Depot. I'm sure Ray expressed concern whether Destry would be alright. That would explain whatever strange behavior Ray was exhibiting when he returned. He was just troubled by his cousin's demeanor.

The next morning, he was up early after sleeping in the back of his pickup at the cross. He had nothing to do and couldn't sleep anymore so he likely drove around for awhile, but ultimately went to park at a large apartment complex that was en route to the Depot where he could observe anyone going to or from. About 9:15 a.m., he saw me go by towards the Depot and when I came back around 9:45, so he knew I had switched vehicles and when I became aware of what had happened. It must have been exhilarating, but there was no reason to rush things. He was observed driving around the park where the festival was being held at around 10:15. Eventually he made his way to the restaurant Jessie worked at to get a free meal, somewhere after 11, since it didn't even open until then.

Ray left the restaurant and came to our house to see how the plan was working. Did we think it was a suicide or not? Was his life going to get complicated, or was he once more going to slide by like he always did, by the grace of his silver tongue and fickle luck? He broke down when appropriate with the pastor, just as he had at Adam's funeral. It had served him well enough then. He came inside and spoke of Destry and Nichole driving by the night before and how Destry had smiled and waved. After all, Nichole was a witness to the event and she might tell everyone they saw Ray and Jessie. Nobody would find out about the phone call at 1:07 a.m. that night, so there was no need to bring it up and he didn't, until he had no choice but to three months later.

Postlude

I've presented a factual account of the events surrounding the death of Destry Greer Allen, our son for seventeen years. Everything written about is documented. The names of some of those that helped me were changed, but that's it. I have no illusions that I'm a serious author and I've not tried to portray myself as one. I've kept the story relatively stark by intention. I'm just trying to tell a story I believe deserved to be told.

How did it all end? As parents that have lost children know all too well, the loss is just the beginning. One hears the term closure bantered around quite a bit, but to those in the club, it's just another concept invented by people that don't know what true loss is, who use the term to make themselves feel better. They like to think bad things can be fixed. In our case, the loss, combined with the coordinated attempts by county officials to crush what resolve we had left, the damage has been even more acute. Though catching and punishing Destry's killer would certainly be a welcome turn of events, I doubt it would make getting out of bed any easier on bad days than it is now. Destry's gone. Nothing will change that.

A Pristine Suicide

What happened to Destry? The reader is left to draw their own conclusions. Maybe I'm crazy, certainly considered a possibility among parents that have truly put themselves in my position. Parents that are honest enough with themselves to acknowledge they don't know if they could survive the loss of one of their children at all, much less the abuse by the system we've been subjected to, and that going crazy could be one potential outcome. Maybe I haven't completely lost my mind, but we all know parents of suicide victims are believed to often delude themselves because they don't want to accept the truth. I certainly can acknowledge that would be a possibility for some.

No official from Saline County has ever been in touch with us since we went to them in December of 2004. I did manage to corner the sheriff briefly in two public forums when I ran for the position in 2008, but that was by my initiative and Kochanowski simply lied through his teeth for the benefit of the listeners.

Whatever happened, certain significant facts have to be taken into consideration. No investigation was conducted into Destry's death, a blatant violation of Destry's civil rights, plain and simple, as was the malicious prosecution and persecution by the Salina Police Department and Saline County Prosecutors office. Saline County officials slammed the door in our faces when they found out their negligent behavior had been revealed, something indefensible in court.

Going on the seventh anniversary of Destry's death, Ray and Jessie have never been questioned about the night or why they perjured themselves in court to create an alibi, why they wanted 5th Amendment protection when questioned, and how Ray knew Destry was dead an hour before I called it in. Tommy has never been questioned as to why his mother would tell people his phone was used, he knew what happened, and he feared coming back to Kansas. Ray knew what the crime scene looked like and described it as something that "wouldn't bother a deer hunter." Last, but certainly not least, Destry's death is an open investigation, an unsolved suicide - the ultimate definition of an oxymoron.

Civil liability was the only thing the Saline County was worried about, not letting a killer go. According to the text

185

Constitutional Law, 12th edition by Jaqueline R. Kanovitz, the operative mechanism is Title 42 U.S.C. § 1983, a broadly used federal statute which "imposes civil liability on law enforcement officials who act under the color of the state law in depriving members of the public their constitutional rights." Usually, the defendants are the only ones that are held liable in a § 1983 action for their acts or omissions, not for what anybody else does, such as the department itself. However, the "department and supervisory personnel are also liable if they did or failed to do something that caused the violation to occur, such as by not adequately training or supervising the offending officer." Investigator Smith was certainly not trained or supervised to any meaningful degree by the SO. His priority was taking the weekend off.

Additionally, in the malicious prosecution case we were filing against Saline County, the police chief and county prosecutor, the initial offense was by a rank and file patrolman. However, the major constitutional offense was committed by those above him when his superiors chose to prosecute Destry for a crime they fully knew he didn't commit and that someone else had actually already been convicted of.

Throughout the course of the investigation, only Kim's new wife, Kelly, came to Ray's defense. She had a checkered past herself and wanted nothing to do with Ray actually being in her life. Kelly had her own troublesome kids to worry about. Principally, she was a clone of Jessie. She just liked to fight, even when it wasn't her fight. She had a terrible effect on Kim personally, directly resulting in his termination from the company he had worked at for over fifteen years. When they left town, they didn't want Ray to come and left him here, but for some reason she felt she was in some morally superior position to defend Ray. Her arguments made no sense and contained no true facts, since her primary source of information had always been Ray and his cockeyed view of the world. Many of her ramblings, though nearly incoherent, seemed to justify whatever Ray might have done as being deserved. I personally would rather have no one come forward to defend me than a person of Kelly's ilk. Nonetheless, she was all alone in his corner.

I've tried hard to stay away from the personal side of the story. That's at least a whole other book in itself. However, there is one aspect I feel compelled to comment on. I've referred to television's portrayal of certain situations throughout this book, not as points of factual representation, but rather as one of the main points of reference for the general population. True or not, most of the public have nothing else to compare to. How is a person in my situation typically portrayed? Picture various Mel Gibson characters. They lay painful waste to the offenders, to hell with the consequences. Of course, the producers always conveniently forget to show those consequences.

In fact, in my case, I was forced to persuade two people, who felt strongly about right and wrong, out of making Ray disappear. They had known Destry, were eager to help and were what I have always considered good people. I still do. For me, it was never a difficult decision not to do the wrong thing. At the end of the day, I am not a murderer, plain and simple. I'm not a follower of the darkness. I prefer to live in the light. I love my family and spend most of my time trying to make the most of every second I have left on this earth in some useful fashion. I spend my time trying to doing things that matter, like writing this book.

We don't waste our time chasing happiness anymore, or anything else, for that matter. Happiness, or even survival, exists only in the moment. Destry taught us to appreciate what we have right now, this second. Do you love someone? Tell them soon and tell them often. They're likely to die before you think they should. There is no control, there is no tomorrow. They're just seductive illusions.

When was the last time you saw a movie about the guy whose son was murdered, the authorities got in his way, and he did the right thing, the smart thing? That tried to salvage what family and life was left, to get justice without going to prison for the rest of his life and decimating what little family and finances were left? I've never heard of that movie. I'd be surprised if anyone even wanted to see it. If I had given Ray Jones what he deserved, one hundred percent of the people I've talked to think

I would've been well within my rights to do so. After all, that's what they do on television, and in parts of the Bible I might add.

That brings up a point that we've always found of interest. Destry's story, exclusive of the bastardization of the legal process, is very reminiscent of the tale of Cane and Abel out of the Bible. Not to be overly simplistic or offensive, but Abel was killed by Cane because what Abel had to offer was more desirable and Cane became envious. Destry, a modern version of Abel, was liked and respected by many and his work was appreciated, as opposed to Ray, the new Cane. What Destry had to offer, honest friendship and trust, was more desirable, and Ray killed him out of jealousy.

I mention this not because I'm religious, but because when I relate the story of Destry's death to people, I find they're often hesitant to believe me. This is despite the fact we live in the Bible belt and the book is taken literally by many. Religious or not, the fact people have been killed for jealousy since time began would be the relevant point. People sit and watch crime dramas, consistently the most popular shows on television, but for some reason don't grasp the fact that such things happen here too, not just somewhere else or in the imagination. I don't really blame them. I used to be just the same. Bad things only happened to other people, somewhere else.

Lastly, a thought provoking bit of irony. Theresa and I used to watch a lot of old movies when we first got together. Jimmy Stewart, whose on-screen portrayals were often men of honor and character, was a favorite of ours and came to influence our choice of names for two of the three Allen boys. *Destry Rides Again* was a popular Western comedy spoof written about Thomas Jefferson Destry. In the 1939 version, Jimmy Stewart stars as Destry, the son of a legendary frontier peacekeeper who is hired as the new deputy to tame a lawless town – but he doesn't carry a gun. Predictably enough, he prevails in the end. In Destry Allen's version of *Destry Rides Again*, he was the son of the not yet elected sheriff and, unfortunately, the bad guy did carry a gun, and won – at least for the time being.

From *Constitutional Law,* 12ᵗʰ edition, by Jacqueline R. Kanovitz:

"*Twentieth Century America has a right to demand for itself, and the obligation to secure for its citizens, law enforcement personnel whose conduct is above and beyond reproach. The police officer is expected to conduct himself lawfully and properly to bring honor and respect to the law which he is sworn and bound to uphold. He who fails to so comport brings upon the law grave shadows of public distrust. We demand from our law enforcement officers, and properly so, adherence to demanding standards which are higher than those applied in many other professions. It is a standard which demands more than forbearance from overt and indictable illegal conduct. It demands that in both an officer's private and official lives he do nothing to bring dishonor upon his noble calling and in no way contribute to a weakening of the public confidence and trust.*"

Cerceo v. Darby, 281 A.2d 251,255 (Pa. 1971)